TOWER HAMLETS
91 000 004 502 07 6
200 e
akes
D0618825

hamlyn | all colour cookbook

200 easy cakes & bakes

Joanna Farrow

An Hachette UK Company
www.hachette.co.uk

First published in Great Britain in 2013 by
Hamlyn, a division of Octopus Publishing Group Ltd
Endeavour House 189 Shaftesbury Avenue
London WC2H 8JY
www.octopusbooks.co.uk

Some of the recipes in this book have previously appeared in other books published by Hamlyn.

ISBN 978-0-600-62530-8

A CIP catalogue record for this book is available from the British Library

Printed and bound in China

1 2 3 4 5 6 7 8 9 10

Both metric and imperial measurements have been given in all recipes. Use one set of measurements only, and not a mixture of both.

Standard level spoon measurements are used in all recipes.
1 tablespoon = one 15 ml spoon
1 teaspoon = one 5 ml spoon

Ovens should be preheated to the specified temperature – if using a fan-assisted oven, follow the manufacturer's instructions for adjusting the time and the temperature.

Fresh herbs should be used unless otherwise stated.
Medium eggs should be used unless otherwise stated.

The Department of Health advises that eggs should not be consumed raw. This book contains some dishes made with raw or lightly cooked eggs. It is prudent for vulnerable people such as pregnant and nursing mothers, invalids, the elderly, babies and young children to avoid uncooked or lightly cooked dishes made with eggs. Once prepared, these dishes should be kept refrigerated and used promptly.

This book includes dishes made with nuts and nut derivatives. It is advisable for those with known allergicreactions to nuts and nut derivatives and those who may be potentially vulnerable to these allergies, such as pregnant and nursing mothers, invalids, the elderly, babies and children, to avoid dishes made with nuts and nut oils. It is also prudent to check the labels of pre-prepared ingredients for the possible inclusion of nut derivatives.

contents

introduction

introduction

Of all the different types of cooking, baking continues to thrive as the one we love most. It's a fun, enjoyable way to spend a bit of time and appeals to all ages; even kids love it! It's not difficult to see why baking has such enduring popularity. Not only does it produce comfort food at its best (who doesn't like a wedge of chocolate cake?), it's also inexpensive and doesn't require advanced culinary knowledge or a kitchen packed with special equipment. It's fascinating to think that by simply whisking together such basic ingredients as butter, sugar, eggs and flour, we can transform them into something that tastes so good. Add a few extra ingredients – fruit, spices, chocolate and vanilla to name but a few – and it gets even better. Feast your eyes on the wealth of recipes in this book, make a cup of tea and get baking!

equipment

You've probably already got most of the equipment needed to bake a cake. A few tins, bowls and a whisk is really all you need to get started.

cake tins

Deep-sided cake tins are useful for simple fruit cakes, sponge cakes and Madeira cakes. Both fixed- or loose-bottomed ones can be used for the recipes in this book. The main advantage of loose-bottomed tins, in which the cake is removed by pushing the base up through the tin, is that they enable fragile sponges to be removed easily from the tin, eliminating the risk of damage that inverting them out of the tin might cause. Fixed-bottomed tins are fine for firmer sponges and fruit cakes. Spring-form cake tins can be used as long as the cake isn't too deep.

If you'd prefer to bake a square cake, the tin size should be 2.5 cm (1 inch) smaller than a round cake tin. For example, use an 18 cm (7 inch) square tin instead of a 20 cm (8 inch) round one. For how to line cake tins, see pages 12–15.

sandwich tins

Useful for Victoria sandwich cakes, carrot and chocolate sandwich cakes, these can be fixed- or loose-bottomed. Buy ones that are at least 3.5 cm (1½ inches) deep so that the sponge doesn't rise over the sides.

loaf tins

These vary hugely in size and capacity. The teabread recipes in this book provide both a weight and capacity for the tin in case you're not sure of the size of your loaf tin.

cupcake and muffin trays

Twelve-hole cupcake and muffin trays vary in size, including the small ones you'd use to bake jam tarts or fairy cakes in. The recipes in this book are made using slightly larger trays, the sort you'd make individual Yorkshire puddings in.

paper cake cases

These come in a huge range of sizes, from the little fairy cake cases to large muffin ones. In the supermarkets, specialist cake shops and online sources, you'll find a good range of colours and patterns and they might be labelled cupcake, muffin or cake cases. The recipes in this book are designed for cases that are larger than a fairy cake case but a little smaller than a large muffin case. (If you opened one out and flattened it on the work surface, it should measure about 12 cm (5 inches) in diameter).

baking sheets

A couple of baking sheets are useful for baking cookies, scones and meringues as well as savoury bakes. Some have one lipped edge to make them easier to grip, while others have a shallow-lipped edge all round. Either can be used for the recipes in this book, although it's worth having a flat-edged (non-lipped) baking sheet for items that you want to slide off once cooked.

mixing bowls

Collect a range of bowls in various sizes so they're easy to store and suit varying amounts of ingredients to be mixed. A large bowl is ideal for vigorous mixing of cake ingredients or egg whites, while smaller bowls are suitable for creams, fillings, icings and frostings.

Metal bowls are easy to manage and enduring. Glass or plastic ones are useful for softening butter in the microwave prior to adding the remaining cake or icing ingredients.

whisks and mixers

Use a hand-held electric whisk or free-standing electric mixer for mixing and beating. A wooden spoon can be used instead but can be hard work, particularly for blending cake mixtures. Hand-held electric whisks are inexpensive and make really light work of cake making.

measuring scales

Kitchen scales, whether balance or digital, are essential for cake making, as weighing out the right quantities is the only way to ensure good results. The advantage with digital scales is that you can place a bowl or pan directly on the scales and add the ingredients to it.

plastic spatulas

Flexible and hard wearing, these are great for scraping out all the mixture from a bowl so that nothing gets wasted. They can also be used instead of a wooden spoon for beating mixtures.

palette knife

Although not essential, a small palette knife is great for spreading icings and frostings over cakes.

lining tins

Refer to your chosen recipe to see whether the tin needs lining. Some only require base-lining, others both base and sides. Don't forget to grease the paper once you've lined the tin. Without this the cake mixture will stick to the paper and won't rise.

greaseproof versus baking parchment

Greaseproof paper is generally used for lining cake tins, loaf tins and the bases of sandwich tins. It is not as strong as baking parchment, which must be used for lining baking sheets for meringues. If you bake meringues on a greaseproof-lined baking sheet they will stick!

paper cake liners

Cake tin liners resembling giant paper muffin cases are available in various sizes and can be used to fit into loaf tins and round cake tins. There's no need to grease the tin or the liners.

reusable baking liner

This is a strong, nonstick liner that comes on a roll and can be cut to fit cake tins and baking sheets. It's more expensive than paper but is washable, long-lasting and dispenses with the need to grease.

how to line a...

sandwich tin

Draw around the tin on a double-thickness piece of greaseproof paper and cut out two circles. Grease the tin and press the paper into the base. Grease the paper. Tip a little flour to one side of the tin and tilt the tin so that the flour dusts the side. Shake out the excess.

round cake tin

Draw around the tin on a piece of greaseproof paper and cut out the circle. Cut strips of paper that are slightly wider than the height of the tin. Fold over a 1.5 cm (¾ inch) lip along one edge and snip it at intervals to the fold. Brush the base

and side of the tin with melted butter. Fit the paper strip around the side so that the snipped edge sits on the base. Finish lining the side, then press the circle of paper on to the base. Grease the paper.

square cake tin
Use the same technique as for a round tin but snip the strip to make the paper fit only at the corners of the tin.

loaf tin
Cut out a wide strip of paper that's long enough to cover the base and long sides of the tin and overhang the sides slightly. Grease the base and sides of the tin, then press the strip into the tin to cover the base and long sides. Grease the paper. Once the cake is baked, loosen it at the short ends of the tin with a knife and then lift the cake out by holding the ends of the greaseproof strip.

shallow baking or roasting tin
Grease the base and sides of the tin. Cut out a rectangle of greaseproof paper that's at least 10 cm (4 inches) longer and wider than the size of the tin. Press the paper down into the tin. Snip the paper at the corners so that you can fit the paper neatly around the sides of the tin. Grease the paper.

techniques

Take a few moments to check out the following techniques, particularly if you've never baked before. You'll pick up a few tips that will help you to produce perfect results whatever the recipe.

softening and melting butter
Most cake recipes require softened butter in order to blend easily with other ingredients to make a smooth, creamy mixture. Even at room temperature butter can still be quite firm, so the best way to soften it quickly is to use the microwave. Cut the measured butter into small pieces in a bowl. Microwave on medium power in short spurts until the butter is soft enough to be pushed into with your finger. Don't leave it too long or the butter will melt. For melting butter to grease tins or for the few recipes that require melted butter, melt the measured butter in

the same way (or just a knob of butter for greasing), watching closely as it'll start to splutter if left too long.

mixing a basic sponge

Most of the recipes in this book use the 'all-in-one' method of cake making in which the sponge ingredients are put in a bowl in one go and beaten until smooth and creamy. Make sure you've softened the butter first and ideally use an electric whisk for beating. The mixture is ready once it looks smooth and creamy and is paler in colour. This will take 1–2 minutes with an electric whisk or about 5 minutes if using a wooden spoon. Scrape the mixture down from the side of the bowl with a plastic spatula as you work.

filling paper cases

Avoid over-filling cupcake cases with the mixture, as they'll spill over the sides and will be spoilt. Spoon in the mixture so that it fills each case about two-thirds full. (It might take a couple of bakes to get it just right). For muffins, you can pile in the mixture a little more, as it tends to be firmer and will rise up higher.

testing whether cakes are cooked

About 5 minutes before the end of the cooking time for a large cake (or a couple of minutes for a small cake), carefully open the oven door to see whether it's cooked. If the surface of the cake looks cooked and is firm and spongy when gently pressed with your

fingers it's most likely ready. For recipes that require testing with a skewer, gently press the skewer into the centre of the cake and pull out slowly. There should be no uncooked mixture on the skewer – it should look clean. If the cake isn't ready, pop it back for a few minutes more. Always avoid opening an oven door too much, as the influx of cool air might cause the cake to deflate.

cooling cakes

Some cakes, such as chocolate brownies, fruit cakes or delicate sponges, are left to cool in the tin otherwise they might break up as you try to turn them out. Most others are transferred to a wire rack to cool. If the tin is not lined with paper, loosen the edges with a sharp knife before transferring to a wire rack. Cool completely before decorating.

melting chocolate

To melt on the hob, chop the chocolate into small pieces and put in a heatproof bowl. Rest the bowl over a pan of very gently simmering water, making sure the base of the bowl doesn't come in contact with the water. Once the chocolate starts to melt, turn off the heat and leave until completely melted, stirring once or twice until no lumps remain. It's crucial that no water (for example, steam from the pan) gets into the bowl while the chocolate is melting or the chocolate will solidify and cannot be melted again.

To melt in the microwave, chop the chocolate into small pieces and put in a

microwave-proof bowl. Melt the chocolate in 1 minute spurts, checking frequently. Take care, particularly when melting white chocolate or milk chocolate, as these have a higher sugar content and are more prone to scorching.

Sometimes chocolate is melted with other ingredients such as butter or milk. Because of the high fat contents of these additional ingredients, the melting time will be reduced.

storing and freezing cakes

Most cakes are best eaten freshly baked or within 24 hours of making. Muffins and scones are always best on the day they're made, unless you want to make a large quantity for freezing. In which case, thaw them at room temperature for a few hours, then warm them through in a moderate oven for about 5–10 minutes to refresh.

Sponge cakes, including sponge-based teabreads and cupcakes, have a soft, open texture if served on the day they're made but can be successfully stored for 1–2 days in an airtight container, either iced or un-iced. Sponge cakes are also easier to slice if stored overnight, as their texture firms up slightly.

Cakes that include a lot of dried fruit such as a fruity teabread will keep well for several days, while a rich fruit cake will keep for several weeks. Cookies gradually lose their 'snap' during storage and can be crisped up by popping them back in a moderate oven for about 5 minutes. Meringues store well for 3–4 days.

Always store cakes and bakes in an airtight container in a cool place. Don't use the fridge because the cake or bake texture will be spoilt. For cakes that are decorated with cream cheese frosting or whipped cream, you might have to resort to using the fridge during warm weather.

Cakes and bakes can be frozen in a rigid container to avoid damage. If space is tight, 'open freeze' them first (without a container or wrapping) until solid, then wrap in clingfilm or a place in a large freezer bag. Remember to remove from the bag or wrapping before thawing. Cakes can be frozen successfully for several months.

big cakes

citrus spiced madeira cake

Cuts into **10**
Preparation time **15 minutes**
Cooking time **50 minutes**

4 **star anise**, broken into pieces
175 g (6 oz) **caster sugar**
175 g (6 oz) **slightly salted butter**, softened
3 **eggs**
finely grated rind of 1 **orange**
2 tablespoons **orange juice**
250 g (8 oz) **self-raising flour**
1 teaspoon **baking powder**
small piece of **candied orange peel**, cut into thin strips

Put the star anise and 50 g (2 oz) of the sugar in a small food processor, blender or coffee grinder and grind until the star anise is completely ground and the sugar is flecked with colour.

Tip into a bowl, add the butter, remaining sugar, eggs, orange rind and juice, flour and baking powder and beat together until pale and creamy. Spoon the mixture into a greased and lined 18 cm (7 inch) round cake tin (see pages 13–15) and level the surface.

Place the strips of candied peel on the centre of the cake. Bake in a preheated oven, 160°C (325°F), Gas Mark 3, for about 50 minutes or until just firm to the touch and a skewer inserted into the centre comes out clean. Loosen the edge, turn out on to a wire rack and peel off the lining paper. Leave to cool.

For marzipan Madeira cake, make the cake as above, omitting the star anise and reducing the caster sugar to 125 g (4 oz). Dice 200 g (7 oz) white or golden marzipan and stir half into the cake mixture. Spoon into the tin, omitting the candied peel, and scatter with the remaining marzipan. Bake as above.

victoria sandwich cake

Cuts into **8**
Preparation time **15 minutes**
Cooking time **25 minutes**

- 175 g (6 oz) **slightly salted butter**, softened
- 175 g (6 oz) **caster sugar**, plus extra for sprinkling
- 3 **eggs**
- 175 g (6 oz) **self-raising flour**
- 1 teaspoon **baking powder**
- 1 teaspoon **vanilla bean paste** or **extract**
- 1–2 tablespoons **milk**

For the filling

- 150 ml (1/4 pint) **double cream**
- 5 tablespoons **raspberry** or **strawberry jam**

Beat together the butter, sugar, eggs, flour, baking powder and vanilla in a bowl until pale and creamy. Stir in a little milk so that the mixture drops easily from a wooden spoon when tapped against the side of the bowl.

Divide the mixture evenly between 2 greased, base-lined and floured 18 cm (7 inch) sandwich tins (see page 13) and level the surface. Bake in a preheated oven, 180°C (350°F), Gas Mark 4, for about 25 minutes or until risen and just firm to the touch. Loosen the edges, turn out on to a wire rack and peel off the lining paper. Leave to cool.

Make the filling. Whip double cream in a bowl until just holding its shape. Sandwich the cakes together using the jam and cream. Serve sprinkled generously with caster sugar.

For iced ginger cake, make the cakes as above, adding 2 finely chopped pieces of stem ginger in syrup to the cake mixture. For the filling, beat together 50 g (2 oz) softened unsalted butter and 75 g (3 oz) sifted icing sugar until smooth and creamy, then use to sandwich the cooled cakes together. Mix together 150 g (5 oz) sifted icing sugar, 3 tablespoons ginger syrup from the jar and a dash of water to make a smooth, spoonable icing. Spread over the top of the cake so that the icing runs down the side.

toffee chocci cake

Cuts into **10**
Preparation time **20 minutes**
Cooking time **45 minutes**

175 g (6 oz) **plain flour**
25 g (1 oz) **cocoa powder**
½ teaspoon **bicarbonate of soda**
½ teaspoon **baking powder**
200 g (7 oz) **light muscovado sugar**
1 **egg**
4 tablespoons **milk**
1 teaspoon **vanilla extract**
65 g (2½ oz) **slightly salted butter**, diced
100 g (3½ oz) **plain dark chocolate**, chopped
125 ml (4 fl oz) **water**
chocolate curls, to decorate

For the topping
40 g (1½ oz) very soft **unsalted butter**
200 g (7 oz) **ready-made caramel** or **toffee sauce** (see right for homemade)

Mix together the flour, cocoa powder, bicarbonate of soda, baking powder and sugar in a bowl. Beat together the egg, milk and vanilla in a small bowl.

Put the butter, chocolate and measurement water in a saucepan and heat very gently, stirring frequently, until melted and smooth. Add the egg mixture and melted butter and chocolate mixture to the dry ingredients and stir well to mix.

Spoon the mixture into a greased and lined 23 cm (9 inch) round or 20 cm (8 inch) square cake tin (see pages 13–15) and level the surface. Bake in a preheated oven, 180°C (350°F), Gas Mark 4, for 30–40 minutes until just firm to the touch and a skewer inserted into the centre comes out clean. Loosen the edges, turn out on to a wire rack and peel off the lining paper. Leave to cool.

Make the topping. Beat together the butter and caramel or toffee sauce (see below) in a bowl. Transfer the cake to a serving plate, spread the topping over the top of the cake and scatter with chocolate curls.

For homemade toffee sauce, put 5 tablespoons water and 200 g (7 oz) caster or granulated sugar in a small saucepan and heat very gently, stirring occasionally, until the sugar dissolves. Bring to the boil and boil without stirring for about 5 minutes or until a golden caramel (watch closely to avoid burning). Dip the base of the pan in cold water to stop further cooking. Add 50 g (2 oz) slightly salted butter and 3 tablespoons double cream, return to the heat and stir until softened and smooth. Leave to cool.

easy simnel cake

Cuts into **16**
Preparation time **25 minutes**, plus cooling
Cooking time **2–2½ hours**

175 g (6 oz) **slightly salted butter**, softened
175 g (6 oz) **light muscovado sugar**
2 teaspoons **ground ginger**
2 teaspoons **ground mixed spice**
3 **eggs**
225 g (7½ oz) **plain flour**
2 teaspoons **vanilla extract**
500 g (1 lb) **luxury mixed dried fruit**
500 g (1 lb) **white** or **golden marzipan**
1 **egg white**, lightly beaten, for brushing
yellow flowers, such as roses, or **rose petals**, to decorate
sifted **icing sugar**, for dusting

Beat together the butter, muscovado sugar, ginger, mixed spice, eggs, flour and vanilla in a bowl until smooth and creamy. Stir in the dried fruit until evenly combined. Spoon half the mixture into a greased and lined 18 cm (7 inch) round cake tin (see pages 13–15) and level the surface.

Roll out half the marzipan on a surface lightly dusted with sifted icing sugar into a round the same size as the tin. Press into the tin and cover with the remaining mixture. Level the surface. Bake in a preheated oven, 150°C (300°F), Gas Mark 2, for 2–2½ hours or until a skewer inserted into the centre comes out clean. Leave to cool in the tin.

Transfer the cake to a baking sheet, peel off the lining paper and brush the top with the egg white. Roll out the remaining marzipan until slightly larger than the top of the cake. Lift over the cake and press down gently. Pinch the edges of the marzipan to decorate.

Brush with a little more egg white and cook under a preheated grill until lightly toasted, turning the cake if necessary to evenly colour. Leave to cool. Decorate with flowers or rose petals and dust with sifted icing sugar.

For Dundee cake, mix together 250 g (8 oz) sultanas, 150 g (5 oz) raisins, 50 g (2 oz) finely chopped candied peel and 50 g (2 oz) ground almonds. Make the cake as above, omitting the spices and adding the sultana mixture instead of the mixed dried fruit. Spoon into the tin, omitting the marzipan, and level the surface. Arrange 40 g (1½ oz) blanched almonds over the top of the cake and bake as above.

carrot sandwich cake

Cuts into **12**
Preparation time **25 minutes**
Cooking time **30 minutes**

175 g (6 oz) **slightly salted butter**, softened
175 g (6 oz) **light muscovado sugar**
3 **eggs**
225 g (7½ oz) **self-raising flour**
2 teaspoons **baking powder**
2 teaspoons **ground mixed spice**
75 g (3 oz) **ground almonds**, **hazelnuts** or **walnuts**
200 g (7 oz) **carrots**, finely grated
75 g (3 oz) **sultanas**

For the frosting
300 g (10 oz) **cream cheese**
75 g (3 oz) **unsalted butter**, softened
100 g (3½ oz) **icing sugar**, sifted, plus extra for dusting
2 teaspoons **lemon juice**

Beat together the butter, sugar, eggs, flour, baking powder, mixed spice and ground nuts in a bowl until smooth and creamy. Stir in the carrots and sultanas until evenly combined.

Divide the mixture evenly between 2 greased, base-lined and floured 20 cm (8 inch) sandwich tins (see page 13) and level the surface. Bake in a preheated oven, 180°C (350°F), Gas Mark 4, for about 30 minutes or until risen and just firm to the touch. Loosen the edges, turn out on to a wire rack and peel off the lining paper. Leave to cool.

Make the frosting. Beat together the cream cheese and butter in a bowl until smooth. Stir in the icing sugar and lemon juice, then use half to sandwich the cakes together. Spread the remaining icing over the top of the cake.

For banana frosting, to use instead of the cream cheese frosting, mash together 2 ripe bananas and 1 teaspoon lemon juice in a bowl to make a loose purée. Press through a sieve into a bowl, scraping the purée that clings to the underside of the sieve into the bowl. Add 200 ml (7 fl oz) extra-thick double cream and 25 g (1 oz) sifted icing sugar and beat well until the mixture holds its shape.

upside-down pineapple cake

Cuts into **8**
Preparation time **30 minutes**
Cooking time **35 minutes**

1 small **ripe pineapple**
3 pieces of **stem ginger in syrup**, chopped
125 g (4 oz) **polenta**
1 teaspoon **baking powder**
125 g (4 oz) **ground almonds**
175 g (6 oz) **slightly salted butter**, softened
175 g (6 oz) **caster sugar**
finely grated rind of 3 **limes**
2 **eggs**, beaten

For the syrup
50 g (2 oz) **caster sugar**
3 tablespoons **water**
juice of 3 **limes**
3 tablespoons **stem ginger syrup**

Cut away the skin from the pineapple and cut the flesh into 1 cm (½ inch) slices. Chop into small pieces, discarding the core. Mix together the pineapple and chopped ginger, then scatter in a greased and base-lined 20 cm (8 inch) round cake tin at least 4.5 cm (1¾ inches) deep (see pages 13–15).

Mix together the polenta, baking powder and ground almonds in a bowl. Beat together the butter, sugar and lime rind in a bowl until pale and creamy. Gradually beat in the eggs. Add the dry ingredients and mix well.

Spoon the mixture into the tin and level the surface. Bake in a preheated oven, 180°C (350°F), Gas Mark 4, for about 35 minutes or until risen, just firm to the touch and a skewer inserted into the centre comes out clean.

Meanwhile, make the syrup. Put the sugar and measurement water in a small saucepan and heat gently until the sugar dissolves. Bring to the boil and boil for about 3 minutes or until thickened. Remove from the heat and stir in the lime juice and ginger syrup.

Loosen the edge of the cake and invert on to a serving plate, peeling off the lining paper. Spoon the syrup over the top and serve warm or cold.

For polenta drizzle cake, make the cake mixture as above, omitting the pineapple, ginger and lime rind and adding ¼ teaspoon ground cloves. Spoon into a greased 23 cm (9 inch) spring-form cake tin and bake as above. Mix together 5 tablespoons clear honey and 4 tablespoons lemon juice. Drizzle over the cake and serve warm or cold with whipped cream or Greek yogurt.

passion fruit bundt cake

Cuts into **10**
Preparation time **30 minutes**
Cooking time **40 minutes**

100 g (3½ oz) **slightly salted butter**, softened
175 g (6 oz) **caster sugar**
2 **eggs**, beaten
1 tablespoon **vanilla extract**
175 ml (6 fl oz) **buttermilk**
200 g (7 oz) **self-raising flour**
1 teaspoon **baking powder**

For the icing
2–3 ripe **passion fruit**
about 125 g (4 oz) **icing sugar**, sifted

Beat together the butter and sugar in a bowl until very pale and creamy. Gradually beat in the eggs. Add the vanilla and buttermilk, then sift in the flour and baking powder. Gently stir together until just combined.

Spoon the mixture into a greased and floured 1.4 litre (2¼ pint) ring mould (see How to Line a Sandwich Tin, page 13) and level the surface. Bake in a preheated oven, 160°C (325°F), Gas Mark 3, for about 40 minutes until risen, just firm to the touch and a skewer inserted into the centre comes out clean. Loosen the edge and turn out on to a wire rack to cool.

Make the icing. Halve and scoop out the pulp from 2 of the passion fruit into a sieve resting over a small bowl. Press the pulp through the sieve, then measure out 4–5 teaspoons of the juice, pulping the third passion fruit if necessary. Stir in enough of the icing sugar to make a smooth, spoonable icing. Spread over the top of the cake so that it runs down the side.

For coffee bundt cake, dissolve 1 tablespoon instant espresso coffee powder or granules in 1½ tablespoons boiling water. Make the cake as above, replacing the vanilla extract with the coffee. For the icing, beat together 125 g (4 oz) sifted icing sugar and 2½–3 tablespoons single cream to make a smooth icing. Spoon over the cooled cake and scatter the top with chopped chocolate-coated coffee beans.

chocolate & coconut cake

Cuts into **12**
Preparation time **30 minutes**
Cooking time **35 minutes**

250 g (8 oz) **plain dark chocolate**, broken into pieces
75 ml (3 fl oz) **water**
175 g (6 oz) **slightly salted butter**, softened
250 g (8 oz) **dark muscovado sugar**
4 **eggs**
100 g (3½ oz) **self-raising flour**
50 g (2 oz) **cocoa powder**
100 g (3½ oz) **ground almonds**
coconut shavings or **shreds**, to decorate (optional)

For the frosting
5 tablespoons **single cream**
50 g (2 oz) **creamed coconut**, roughly chopped
275 g (9 oz) **icing sugar**, sifted
2 teaspoons **lime juice**

Melt the chocolate with the measurement water in a heatproof bowl set over a saucepan of gently simmering water (don't let the base of the bowl touch the water). Beat together the remaining cake ingredients in a large bowl until smooth and creamy. Stir in the melted chocolate.

Divide the mixture evenly between 2 greased and base-lined 20 cm (8 inch) sandwich tins (see page 13) and level the surface. Bake in a preheated oven, 180°C (350°F), Gas Mark 4, for about 30 minutes or until risen and just firm to the touch. Loosen the edges, turn out on to a wire rack and peel off the lining paper. Leave the cakes to cool.

Make the frosting. Put the cream and creamed coconut into a small saucepan and heat gently until the coconut has melted. Turn into a bowl, then beat in the icing sugar and lime juice until smooth. Use half the frosting to sandwich the cakes together. Spread the remaining frosting over the top. Decorate with coconut shavings or shreds, if liked.

For chocolate & hazelnut cake, lightly toast 100 g (3½ oz) hazelnuts under a preheated hot grill, then whizz in a food processor until finely ground. Make the cakes as above, replacing the ground almonds with the hazelnuts. Sandwich the cooled cakes together with 125 g (4 oz) chocolate hazelnut spread, then spread a further 125 g (4 oz) chocolate hazelnut spread over the top. Scatter with roughly chopped toasted hazelnuts to decorate.

flourless chocolate cake

Cuts into **12**
Preparation time **25 minutes**
Cooking time **1 hour**

125 g (4 oz) **blanched almonds**, roughly chopped
125 g (4 oz) **Brazil nuts**, roughly chopped
225 g (7½ oz) **plain dark chocolate**, chopped into 5 mm (¼ inch) pieces
225 g (7½ oz) **slightly salted butter**, softened
4 **eggs**, separated
225 g (7½ oz) **golden caster sugar**
sifted **cocoa powder**, for dusting

Put the almonds, Brazil nuts and chocolate in a food processor and process until the consistency of ground almonds. Beat together the butter, egg yolks and 175 g (6 oz) of the sugar in a bowl until pale and creamy. Stir in the chocolate mixture.

Whisk the egg whites in a large clean bowl with a hand-held electric whisk until peaking. Gradually whisk in the remaining sugar, a spoonful at a time. Stir a quarter of the mixture into the creamed mixture using a large metal spoon. Add the remaining egg whites and stir gently to mix.

Spoon the mixture into a greased and lined 23 cm (9 inch) loose-bottomed or spring-form cake tin (see pages 13–15) and level the surface. Bake in a preheated oven, 160°C (325°F), Gas Mark 3, for about 1 hour or until just firm to the touch and a skewer inserted into the centre comes out clean.

Leave to cool in the tin (the centre of the cake will sink slightly), then remove the ring and base and dust with sifted cocoa powder. Serve with Fresh Raspberry Compote, if liked (see below).

For fresh raspberry compote, to serve as an accompaniment, put 75 g (3 oz) fresh raspberries, 40 g (1½ oz) caster sugar, 1 teaspoon vanilla extract and 1 tablespoon water in a small saucepan. Cook for about 5 minutes until the raspberries are soft and mushy. Strain through a sieve into a bowl and stir in a further 225 g (7½ oz) raspberries. Mix gently until coated in the sauce. Chill until ready to serve.

lemon drizzle cake

Cuts into **8**
Preparation time **20 minutes**
Cooking time **22–28 minutes**

5 **eggs**
100 g (3½ oz) **caster sugar**
pinch of **salt**
125 g (4 oz) **plain flour**
1 teaspoon **baking powder**
finely grated rind of 1 **lemon**
1 tablespoon **lemon juice**
100 g (3½ oz) **butter**, melted and cooled

For the syrup
250 g (8 oz) **icing sugar**, sifted
125 ml (4 fl oz) **lemon juice**
finely grated rind of 1 **lemon**
seeds scraped from 1 **vanilla pod**

Put the eggs, sugar and salt in a large heatproof bowl set over a saucepan of barely simmering water and beat with a hand-held electric whisk for 2–3 minutes or until it triples in volume and thickens to the consistency of lightly whipped cream. Remove from the heat. Sift in the flour and baking powder, add the lemon rind and juice and drizzle the butter down the side of the bowl. Fold in gently.

Pour the mixture into a greased and lined 22 cm (8½ inch) square cake tin (see page 15). Bake in a preheated oven, 180°C (350°F), Gas Mark 4, for 20–25 minutes or until risen, golden and coming away from the sides of the tin.

Meanwhile, put all the syrup ingredients in a small saucepan and heat gently until the sugar dissolves. Increase the heat and boil rapidly for 4–5 minutes. Set aside to cool a little.

Leave the cake to cool in the tin for 5 minutes, then make holes over the surface with a skewer. Drizzle over two-thirds of the warm syrup. Leave the cake to cool and absorb the syrup. Turn the cake out of the tin and peel off the lining paper. Cut into squares or slices and serve with a heaped spoonful of crème fraîche or soured cream and an extra drizzle of syrup.

For citrus drizzle cake with sorbet, make the cake as above, replacing the lemon rind and juice with the finely grated rind of 1 orange rind and 1 tablespoon orange juice. Serve topped with lemon sorbet.

chocolate truffle cake

Cuts into **8**
Preparation time **15 minutes**
Cooking time **40 minutes**

250 g (8 oz) **plain dark chocolate**, broken into pieces
125 g (4 oz) **unsalted butter**
50 ml (2 fl oz) **double cream**
4 **eggs**, separated
125 g (4 oz) **caster sugar**
2 tablespoons **cocoa powder**, sifted
icing sugar, for dusting

Melt the chocolate, butter and cream together in a heatproof bowl set over a saucepan of gently simmering water. Remove from the heat and leave to cool for 5 minutes.

Whisk the egg yolks with 75 g (3 oz) of the sugar until pale and stir in the cooled chocolate mixture.

Whisk the egg whites in a large clean bowl until softly peaking then whisk in the remaining sugar. Fold into the egg yolk mixture with the sifted cocoa powder until evenly incorporated.

Pour the cake mixture into an oiled and base-lined 23 cm (9 inch) spring-form cake tin that has been lightly dusted all over with a little extra cocoa powder. Bake in a preheated oven, 180°C (350°F), Gas Mark 4, for 35 minutes.

Leave to cool in the tin for 10 minutes then turn out on to a serving plate. Serve in wedges, while still warm, with whipped cream and strawberries.

For chocolate & orange cake with brandied oranges, add the finely grated rind of 1 orange when folding in the icing sugar above. Remove the rind from 3 oranges, cut them into segments and soak in 3 tablespoons brandy and 1 tablespoon clear honey. Serve the oranges with the cake and spoon over crème fraîche.

pear & almond cake

Cuts into **8**
Preparation time **20 minutes**
Cooking time **35 minutes**

125 g (4 oz) **unsalted butter**, softened
125 g (4 oz) **caster sugar**
2 **large eggs**, beaten
50 g (2 oz) **plain flour**, sifted
100 g (3½ oz) **ground almonds**
½ teaspoon **baking powder**
3 **ripe pears**, peeled, halved and cored
50 g (2 oz) **flaked almonds**
sifted **icing sugar**, for dusting

Beat together the butter and caster sugar in a bowl until pale and fluffy. Add the eggs, a little at a time, beating well after each addition. If the mixture starts to curdle, add 1 tablespoon of the flour. Fold in the flour, ground almonds and baking powder using a large metal spoon.

Spoon the mixture into a greased 20 cm (8 inch) spring-form cake tin and level the surface. Arrange the pear halves over the top and bake in a preheated oven, 190°C (375°F), Gas Mark 5, for 25 minutes. Sprinkle the flaked almonds over the top and return to the oven for a further 10 minutes until a skewer inserted into the centre comes out clean.

Leave to cool in the tin, then carefully remove the ring and base and dust with sifted icing sugar. Serve with Mascarpone, Marsala & Orange Cream, if liked (see below).

For mascarpone, Marsala & orange cream, to serve as an accompaniment, whisk together the grated rind of 1 orange and 2 tablespoons orange juice, 2 tablespoons sweet Marsala and 100 g (3½ oz) mascarpone cheese in a bowl. Sweeten with sifted icing sugar to taste.

a very happy birthday cake

Cuts into **12**
Preparation time **25 minutes**
Cooking time **35–40 minutes**

175 g (6 oz) **slightly salted butter**, softened
175 g (6 oz) **caster sugar**
2 teaspoons **vanilla extract**
300 g (10 oz) **self-raising flour**
2 teaspoons **baking powder**
3 **eggs**
50 g (2 oz) **ground rice**
150 ml (1/4 pint) **low-fat natural yogurt**
175 g (6 oz) **strawberries,** hulled and cut into wedges

To finish
300 ml (1/2 pint) **double cream**
3 tablespoons **reduced-sugar strawberry jam**

Put the butter, sugar and vanilla in a food processor and blend until smooth. Sift in the flour and baking powder, add the eggs, ground rice and yogurt and whizz together until creamy.

Divide the mixture between 2 greased and base-lined 20 cm (8 inch) sandwich tins (see page 13) and level the surface. Bake in a preheated oven, 180°C (350°F), Gas Mark 4, for 35–40 minutes until risen, golden and springy to the touch. Leave to cool in the tins for 10 minutes, then turn out on to a wire rack and peel off the lining paper. Leave to cool completely.

Whip the cream in a bowl until soft peaks form. Cut the top off one of the cakes to level it, then spread with the jam and then half of the cream to the edge. Scatter with two-thirds of the strawberries. Place the second cake on top and spread with the remaining cream. Scatter with the remaining strawberries or form them into the birthday girl or boy's initials. Add candles.

For chocolate birthday cake, make the cake as above, replacing 25 g (1 oz) of the flour with 25 g (1 oz) cocoa powder. To fill, omit the jam and spread with the cream. Replace the strawberries with 200 g (7 oz) chocolate-coated honeycomb balls, lightly crushed, and use to fill and decorate the cake.

apple & blackberry crumble cake

Cuts into **16**
Preparation time **30 minutes**
Cooking time **45 minutes**

175 g (6 oz) **butter**, softened
175 g (6 oz) **caster sugar**
3 **eggs**, beaten
200 g (7 oz) **self-raising flour**
1 teaspoon **baking powder**
grated rind of 1 **lemon**
500 g (1 lb) **cooking apples**, cored, peeled and thinly sliced
150 g (5 oz) **frozen blackberries**, just thawed

For the crumble topping
75 g (3 oz) **self-raising flour**
75 g (3 oz) **muesli**
50 g (2 oz) **caster sugar**
75 g (3 oz) **butter**, chilled and diced

Beat together the butter and sugar in a bowl until pale and creamy. Gradually mix in alternate spoonfuls of egg and flour until all has been added and the mixture is smooth. Stir in the baking powder and lemon rind.

Spoon the mixture into a greased and lined 28 x 18 cm (11 x 7 inch) shallow baking tin or roasting tin (see page 15) and level the surface. Arrange the apple slices and blackberries over the top.

Make the crumble topping. Put the flour, muesli and sugar in a bowl or food processor, add the butter and rub in with the fingertips or process until the mixture resembles fine breadcrumbs. Sprinkle over the top of the fruit. Bake in a preheated oven, 180°C (350°F), Gas Mark 4, for about 45 minutes until the crumble is golden brown and a skewer inserted into the centre comes out clean.

Leave to cool in the tin, then transfer to a board. Cut the cake into 16 bars and peel off the lining paper.

For apple & mincemeat crumble cake, make the cake as above, replacing the blackberries with 150 g (5 oz) mincemeat. Sprinkle with the crumble topping, then add 25 g (1 oz) flaked almonds. Bake as above.

sweetie time cake

Cuts into **10**
Preparation time **1 hour**
Cooking time **25 minutes**

175 g (6 oz) **slightly salted butter**, softened
175 g (6 oz) **caster sugar**
3 **eggs**
175 g (6 oz) **self-raising flour**
1 teaspoon **baking powder**
1–2 tablespoons **milk**

For the buttercream
250 g (8 oz) **unsalted butter**, softened
325 g (11 oz) **icing sugar**, sifted
2 teaspoons **vanilla extract**
drop of **pink food colouring**
2 teaspoons **boiling water**

To finish
5 tablespoons **strawberry jam**
200 g (7 oz) **small sweets**, such as **dolly mixtures**
sugar sprinkles

Beat together the butter, sugar, eggs, flour and baking powder in a bowl until pale and creamy. Stir in a little milk so that the mixture drops easily from a wooden spoon when tapped against the side of the bowl.

Divide the mixture evenly between 2 greased, base-lined and floured 18 cm (7 inch) sandwich tins (see page 13) and level the surface. Bake in a preheated oven, 180°C (350°F), Gas Mark 4, for about 25 minutes or until risen and just firm to the touch. Loosen the edges, turn out on to a wire rack and peel off the lining paper. Leave to cool.

Make the buttercream. Beat together the butter and icing sugar in a bowl until pale and creamy. Add the vanilla, pink food colouring and measurement water and beat well. Sandwich the cakes together using the jam and a quarter of the buttercream. Spread the remaining icing over the top and side of the cake. Scatter with the sweets and sugar sprinkles. Add birthday candles, if liked.

For flower garden cake, make the cakes as above. For the buttercream, replace the pink food colouring with a drop of green food colouring. Use to sandwich and cover the cakes. Thinly roll out 75 g (3 oz) each of deep yellow, red and orange ready-to-roll icing on a surface dusted with sifted icing sugar. Cut out small flower shapes with cutters. Arrange over the top of the cake with a handful of ready-made sugar flowers. Pipe coloured dots of icing into the flower centres using tubes of writing icing.

pink heart cake

Cuts into **12**
Preparation time **1 hour**
Cooking time about **1¼ hours**

225 g (7½ oz) **slightly salted butter**, softened
175 g (6 oz) **caster sugar**
3 **eggs**
250 g (9 oz) **self-raising flour**
1 teaspoon **baking powder**
100 g (3½ oz) **ground almonds**
200 g (7 oz) **white chocolate**, chopped into 5 mm (¼ inch) pieces
4 tablespoons **milk**

To finish
5 tablespoons **smooth apricot jam**
750 g (1½ lb) **white ready-to-roll icing**
sifted **icing sugar**, for dusting
2–3 tablespoons **multicoloured sugar sprinkles**

Beat together the butter, sugar, eggs, flour, baking powder and ground almonds in a bowl until pale and creamy. Sprinkle in 175 g (6 oz) of the chocolate, drizzle with the milk and stir gently.

Spoon the mixture into a greased and lined 20 cm (8 inch) round cake tin (see pages 13–15) and level the surface. Bake in a preheated oven, 160°C (325°F), Gas Mark 3, for about 1–1¼ hours or until just firm and a skewer inserted into the centre comes out clean. Turn out on to a wire rack, peel off the lining paper and leave to cool.

Spread the jam over the cake. Roll out the icing on a surface dusted with sifted icing sugar to a 30 cm (12 inch) round. Lift over the cake and fit around the side, easing out the folds and trimming off the excess. Smooth down with hands dusted with icing sugar.

Press a 8 cm (3¼ inch) heart biscuit cutter into the top and lift away the icing inside the cut area. Melt the remaining chocolate (see page 17) and spread into the heart shape, then scatter over the sprinkles. To finish, wrap a pastel-coloured ribbon around the side.

For festive star cake, make the cake as above, replacing the chocolate, if liked, with 200 g (7 oz) chopped natural glacé cherries. Cover the cake with jam. Roll out 250 g (8 oz) white or golden marzipan into a 20 cm (8 inch) round and secure to the top. Cover the cake with icing as above. Cut out a star shape from the icing using a 12 cm (5 inch) star biscuit cutter, leaving the marzipan in place. Scatter 4 tablespoons edible silver balls into the star. Add a red or silver ribbon.

coffee & walnut cake

Cuts into **10**
Preparation time **25 minutes**
Cooking time **25 minutes**

1 tablespoon **instant espresso powder** or **granules**
1 tablespoon **boiling water**
175 g (6 oz) **slightly salted butter**, softened
175 g (6 oz) **golden caster sugar**
3 **eggs**
175 g (6 oz) **self-raising flour**
1 teaspoon **baking powder**
50 g (2 oz) **walnuts**, finely chopped, plus extra **walnut halves** to decorate

For the buttercream
1 teaspoon **instant espresso powder** or **granules**
2 teaspoons **boiling water**
100 g (3½ oz) **unsalted butter**, softened
150 g (5 oz) **golden icing sugar**, sifted

Dissolve the coffee in the measurement water. Beat together the butter, sugar, eggs, flour and baking powder in a bowl until pale and creamy. Beat in the coffee and chopped walnuts.

Divide the mixture evenly between 2 greased, base-lined and floured 18 cm (7 inch) sandwich tins (see page 13) and level the surface. Bake in a preheated oven, 180°C (350°F), Gas Mark 4, for 25 minutes or until just firm to the touch. Loosen the edges, turn out on to a wire rack and peel off the lining paper. Leave to cool.

Make the buttercream. Dissolve the coffee in the measurement water. Beat together the butter, icing sugar and coffee in a bowl until smooth and creamy. Use half the buttercream to sandwich the cakes together, then spread the remaining buttercream over the top and decorate with the walnut halves.

For mocha sandwich cake, make the cakes as above, replacing 25 g (1 oz) of the flour with 25 g (1 oz) cocoa powder and omitting the walnuts. For the buttercream, beat together 75 g (3 oz) softened unsalted butter and 125 g (4 oz) sifted golden icing sugar until smooth and creamy. Beat in 75 g (3 oz) melted plain dark chocolate (see page 17). Use to sandwich and cover the cooled cakes. Scatter chocolate curls over the top of the cake.

summery clementine cake

Cuts into **10**
Preparation time **25 minutes**, plus cooling
Cooking time **1½ hours**

300 g (10 oz) **clementines**
5 **eggs**, separated
200 g (7 oz) **caster sugar**
200 g (7 oz) **ground almonds**
1 teaspoon **baking powder**
400 g (13 oz) **mixed fresh summer fruits**, such as **strawberries**, **raspberries** and **cherries**
sifted **icing sugar**, for dusting

Put the clementines in a saucepan, cover with water and bring to the boil. Reduce the heat to low and cook gently for about 40 minutes until very soft. Drain and leave until cool enough to handle. Quarter and discard any pips. Blend to a purée in a food processor. Turn into a large bowl and beat in the egg yolks, 150 g (5 oz) of the caster sugar, ground almonds and baking powder.

Whisk the egg whites in a large clean bowl with a hand-held electric whisk until peaking. Gradually whisk in the remaining caster sugar, a spoonful at a time. Stir a quarter of the mixture into the clementine mixture using a large metal spoon. Add the remaining egg whites and stir gently to mix.

Spoon the mixture into a greased and base-lined 22–23 cm (8½–9 inch) spring-form cake tin (see pages 13–15) and level the surface. Bake in a preheated oven, 160°C (325°F), Gas Mark 3, for about 50 minutes until just firm to the touch and a skewer inserted into the centre comes out clean.

Leave to cool in the tin, then turn out. Scatter with the summer fruits, dust with sifted icing sugar and serve with Ginger Marmalade Cream, if liked (see below).

For ginger marmalade cream, to serve as an accompaniment, put 5 tablespoons ginger marmalade and 3 tablespoons ginger wine in a saucepan and heat until the marmalade has melted. Strain through a sieve and leave to cool. Whip 150 ml (¼ pint) double cream, the marmalade mixture and a squeeze of lemon or lime juice in a bowl until softly peaking. Turn into a small dish, cover and chill until ready to serve.

teabreads

mango & vanilla muffin slice

Cuts into **8**
Preparation time **20 minutes**
Cooking time **1 hour**

1 small **ripe mango**
225 g (7½ oz) **plain flour**
2 teaspoons **baking powder**
150 g (5 oz) **golden caster sugar**
50 g (2 oz) **porridge oats**
1 **egg**, beaten
175 ml (6 fl oz) **milk**
1 teaspoon **vanilla bean paste** or **extract**
100 g (3½ oz) **slightly salted butter**, melted
vanilla sugar, for sprinkling

Halve the mango each side of the flat central stone. Cut away the stone, then peel and dice the flesh into 5 mm (¼ inch) pieces.

Sift the flour and baking powder into a bowl, then stir in the caster sugar and oats. Beat together the egg, milk, vanilla and melted butter in a jug. Add to the dry ingredients with half the mango and stir together using a large metal spoon until just combined.

Spoon the mixture into a greased and lined 1 kg (2 lb) or 1.3 litre (2¼ pint) loaf tin (see page 15). Scatter with the remaining mango pieces and bake in a preheated oven, 180°C (350°F), Gas Mark 4, for about 1 hour or until well risen, firm to the touch and a skewer inserted into the centre comes out clean.

Leave to cool in the tin for 5 minutes, then loosen at the ends and transfer to a wire rack to cool. Peel off the lining paper and serve warm or cold, sprinkled with vanilla sugar.

For blueberry breakfast slice, put 75 g (3 oz) chopped dried blueberries and 50 ml (2 fl oz) apple or orange juice in a small saucepan and heat until the juice bubbles, then remove from the heat. Leave to cool until the juice is absorbed. Make the cake as above, omitting the mango and vanilla and adding 1 teaspoon ground cinnamon to the dry ingredients. Stir the blueberries and juice into the cake mixture. Spoon into the tin and sprinkle with 2 tablespoons porridge oats. Bake as above.

date & banana ripple slice

Cuts into **10**
Preparation time **20 minutes**, plus cooling
Cooking time **1 hour 25 minutes**

250 g (8 oz) **stoned dates**, roughly chopped
finely grated rind and juice of **1 lemon**
100 ml (3½ fl oz) **water**
2 small **very ripe bananas**
150 g (5 oz) **slightly salted butter**, softened
150 g (5 oz) **caster sugar**
2 **eggs**
100 ml (3½ fl oz) **milk**
275 g (9 oz) **self-raising flour**
1 teaspoon **baking powder**

Put 200 g (7 oz) of the dates in a small saucepan with the lemon rind and juice and measurement water. Bring to the boil, then reduce the heat and simmer gently for 5 minutes until the dates are soft and pulpy. Mash the mixture with a fork until fairly smooth. Leave to cool.

Mash the bananas to a purée in a bowl, then add the butter, sugar, eggs, milk, flour and baking powder and beat together until smooth.

Spoon a third of the mixture into a greased and lined 1.25 kg (2½ lb) or 1.5 litre (2½ pint) loaf tin (see page 15) and level the surface. Spoon over half the date purée and spread evenly. Add half the remaining cake mixture and spread with the remaining purée. Add the remaining cake mixture and level the surface.

Scatter with the reserved dates and bake in a preheated oven, 160°C (325°F), Gas Mark 3, for about 1 hour 20 minutes or until risen and a skewer inserted into the centre comes out clean. Leave to cool in the tin for 15 minutes, then loosen at the ends and transfer to a wire rack. Peel off the lining paper and leave the cake to cool completely.

For honeyed banana cake, make the cake as above, omitting all the dates. For the honey buttercream, beat together 150 g (5 oz) softened unsalted butter, 6 tablespoons sifted icing sugar and 6 tablespoons clear honey in a bowl until smooth and creamy. Spread over the top of the cooled cake and scatter with dried banana slices, if liked.

poppy seed & apple teabread

Cuts into **10**
Preparation time **20 minutes**, plus cooling
Cooking time about **1¼ hours**

100 g (3½ oz) **dried apples**, roughly chopped
100 ml (3½ fl oz) **water**
175 g (6 oz) **slightly salted butter**, softened
finely grated rind of 2 **lemons**
3 tablespoons **lemon juice**
175 g (6 oz) **caster sugar**
3 **eggs**
250 g (8 oz) **self-raising flour**
50 g (2 oz) **poppy seeds**

For the icing
75 g (3 oz) **icing sugar**, sifted
1 tablespoon **lemon juice**

Put the apples and measurement water in a small saucepan and heat for 5 minutes until the apples have absorbed the water. Leave to cool.

Beat together the remaining cake ingredients in a bowl until pale and creamy. Stir in the cooled apples.

Spoon the mixture into a greased and lined 1 kg (2 lb) or 1.3 litre (2¼ pint) loaf tin (see page 15) and level the surface. Bake in a preheated oven, 160°C (325°F), Gas Mark 3, for 1–1¼ hours or until firm to the touch and a skewer inserted into the centre comes out clean. Loosen the cake at the ends and transfer to a wire rack. Peel off the lining paper and leave to cool.

Make the icing. Beat together the icing sugar and lemon juice in a bowl to make a smooth, spoonable icing. If necessary, add a few drops of water or extra lemon juice. Spoon over the cake so that it runs down the sides.

For frosted orange & poppy seed cake, make the cake as above, replacing the lemon rind and juice with the finely grated rind of 1 orange and 3 tablespoons orange juice. For the frosting, beat 100 g (3½ oz) cream cheese in a bowl to soften. Add 25 g (1 oz) softened unsalted butter, the grated rind of 1 orange, 1 tablespoon orange juice and 50 g (2 oz) sifted icing sugar and beat until smooth. Spread over the top of the cooled cake.

chocolate chip teabread

Cuts into **8**
Preparation time **20 minutes**
Cooking time **50 minutes**

125 g (4 oz) **slightly salted butter**, softened
125 g (4 oz) **light muscovado sugar**
2 **eggs**
125 g (4 oz) **self-raising flour**
25 g (1 oz) **cocoa powder**
150 g (5 oz) **milk chocolate**, chopped into 5 mm (¼ inch) pieces

For the buttercream
50 g (2 oz) **milk chocolate**, broken into pieces
50 g (2 oz) **unsalted butter**, softened
75 g (3 oz) **golden icing sugar**, sifted

Beat together the butter, sugar, eggs, flour and cocoa powder in a bowl until smooth and creamy. Add 125 g (4 oz) of the chopped chocolate to the bowl. Mix well.

Spoon the mixture into a greased and lined 500 g (1 lb) or 750 ml (1¼ pint) loaf tin (see page 15) and level the surface. Bake in a preheated oven, 160°C (325°F), Gas Mark 3, for about 50 minutes or until firm to the touch and a skewer inserted into the centre comes out clean. Loosen the cake at the ends and transfer to a wire rack. Peel off the lining paper and leave to cool.

Make the buttercream. Melt the chocolate in a heatproof bowl set over a saucepan of gently simmering water (don't let the base of the bowl touch the water). Meanwhile, beat together the butter and icing sugar in a bowl until pale and creamy. Beat in the melted chocolate. Spread over the top of the cake and scatter with the reserved chopped chocolate.

For chocolate marble cake, beat together 125 g (4 oz) softened slightly salted butter, 125 g (4 oz) caster sugar, 2 eggs and 150 g (5 oz) self-raising flour in a bowl until smooth. Spoon half the mixture into a separate bowl and stir in 50 g (2 oz) melted plain dark chocolate (see page 17). Place alternate spoonfuls of the 2 mixtures in the tin. Run the tip of a knife through the mixtures to slightly swirl them together. Bake as above. Melt a further 50 g (2 oz) plain dark chocolate and stir in 2 teaspoons golden syrup and 15 g (½ oz) unsalted butter. Stir until melted. Once the mixture thickens slightly, spoon it over the cake, spreading to the edges.

sticky sultana & bran slice

Cuts into **8**
Preparation time **10 minutes**, plus standing
Cooking time **45 minutes**

200 g (7 oz) **sultanas**
125 g (4 oz) **demerara sugar**, plus extra for sprinkling
2 tablespoons **black treacle**
100 g (3½ oz) **shredded bran** or **bran flake** cereal
1 teaspoon **ground mixed spice**
300 ml (½ pint) **milk**
150 g (5 oz) **self-raising flour**

Mix together the sultanas, sugar, treacle, bran, mixed spice and milk in a bowl. Leave to stand for 20 minutes to allow the bran to soften. Stir in the flour.

Tip the mixture into a greased and lined 1 kg (2 lb) or 1.3 litre (2¼ pint) loaf tin (see page 15) and level the surface. Bake in a preheated oven, 160°C (325°F), Gas Mark 3, for about 45 minutes or until risen, firm to the touch and a skewer inserted into the centre comes out clean. Loosen the cake at the ends and transfer to a wire rack. Peel off the lining paper and leave to cool. Cut into slices and spread with a little butter to serve.

For gingered fig slice, make the cake as above, replacing the sultanas with 200 g (7 oz) sliced dried figs, the black treacle with 2 tablespoons clear honey and the mixed spice with 1 piece of stem ginger in syrup, finely chopped. Serve drizzled with extra honey.

chai teabread

Cuts into **10**
Preparation time **15 minutes**, plus standing
Cooking time **1¼ hours**

5 **chai tea bags**
300 ml (½ pint) **boiling water**
250 g (8 oz) **self-raising flour**
1 teaspoon **baking powder**
150 g (5 oz) **light muscovado sugar**
300 g (10 oz) **mixed dried fruit**
50 g (2 oz) **Brazil nuts**, chopped
50 g (2 oz) **butter**
1 **egg**, beaten

Stir the tea bags into the measurement water in a jug and leave to stand for 10 minutes.

Mix together the flour, baking powder, sugar, dried fruit and nuts in a bowl. Remove the tea bags from the water, pressing them against the side of the jug to squeeze out all the water. Thinly slice the butter into the water and stir until melted. Leave to cool slightly. Add to the dry ingredients with the egg and mix together well.

Spoon the mixture into a greased and lined 1 kg (2 lb) or 1.3 litre (2¼ pint) loaf tin (see page 15) and spread the mixture into the corners. Bake in a preheated oven, 160°C (325°F), Gas Mark 3, for 1¼ hours or until risen, firm and a skewer inserted into the centre comes out clean. Loosen the cake at the ends and transfer to a wire rack. Peel off the lining paper and leave to cool. Spread the top with Chai Cream Frosting, if liked (see below).

For chai cream frosting, to spread over the cake, put 50 ml (2 fl oz) milk and 3 chai tea bags in a saucepan and bring to the boil. Remove from the heat and leave the tea bags to infuse in the milk until cold. Discard the tea bags, squeezing them to extract the liquid. Beat together 200 g (7 oz) cream cheese and 25 g (1 oz) very soft unsalted butter in a bowl until smooth. Beat in the flavoured milk and 75 g (3 oz) sifted icing sugar.

pomegranate & ginger slice

Cuts into **20**
Preparation time **25 minutes**
Cooking time **50 minutes**

200 g (7 oz) **plain flour**
1 teaspoon **bicarbonate of soda**
100 ml (3½ fl oz) **milk**
1 **egg**
100 g (3½ oz) **dark muscovado sugar**
125 g (4 oz) **black treacle**
75 g (3 oz) **unsalted butter**
3 pieces of **stem ginger in syrup**, chopped

For the topping
300 ml (½ pint) **pomegranate juice**
2 tablespoons **clear honey**
1 **pomegranate**

Sift the flour and bicarbonate of soda into a bowl. Beat together the milk and egg in a jug. Put the sugar, treacle and butter in a saucepan and heat gently until the butter melts and the sugar dissolves. Remove from the heat and add to the milk mixture with the chopped ginger. Add to the dry ingredients and stir together using a large metal spoon until well combined.

Spoon the mixture into 2 greased and lined 1 kg (2 lb) or 1.3 litre (2¼ pint) loaf tins (see page 15) and level the surface. Bake in a preheated oven, 160°C (325°F), Gas Mark 3, for 30 minutes or until just firm to the touch and a skewer inserted into the centre comes out clean. Leave to cool in the tins, then loosen at the ends and transfer to a wire rack. Peel off the lining paper.

Make the topping. Pour the pomegranate juice into a saucepan and bring to the boil, then boil for about 15 minutes until thick and syrupy and reduced to about 3 tablespoons. Stir in the honey. Halve the pomegranate and push the halves inside out to release the fleshy seeds, discarding any white membrane. Scatter the seeds over the top of the cakes. Drizzle with the syrup and cut into small squares to serve.

For sultana & lemon gingerbread, make the cakes as above, reducing the milk by 25 ml (1 fl oz) and sprinkling 75 g (3 oz) sultanas over the mixture in the tins. For the icing, mix together 75 g (3 oz) sifted golden icing sugar and 2 teaspoons lemon juice in a bowl to make a smooth, spoonable icing, then drizzle in lines over the cooled cakes.

jamaican ginger cake

Cuts into **10**
Preparation time **30 minutes**, plus cooling
Cooking time **55–65 minutes**

150 g (5 oz) **butter**
150 g (5 oz) **golden syrup**
150 g (5 oz) **black treacle**
150 g (5 oz) **plain flour**
150 g (5 oz) **strong wholemeal bread flour**
4 teaspoons **ground ginger**
1 teaspoon **ground mixed spice**
1 teaspoon **bicarbonate of soda**
2 **eggs**, beaten
4 tablespoons **milk**

For the topping
1 tablespoon **apricot jam**
125 g (4 oz) **exotic dried fruit**, cut into strips
1 piece of **stem ginger in syrup**, sliced

Put the butter, golden syrup and treacle in a saucepan and heat gently, stirring occasionally, until the butter has melted. Remove from the heat and leave to cool for 5 minutes.

Mix together all the dry ingredients in a large bowl. Gradually mix in the syrup mixture, then the eggs and milk and beat well until smooth.

Pour into a greased and lined 1 kg (2 lb) or 1.3 litre (2¼ pint) loaf tin (see page 15). Bake in a preheated oven, 160°C (325°F), Gas Mark 3, for 50–60 minutes until well risen, the top has cracked and a skewer inserted into the centre comes out clean.

Leave to cool in the tin for 10 minutes, then loosen at the ends and transfer to a wire rack. Peel off the lining paper and leave to cool completely.

Make the topping. Spread the jam over the top of the cake, then decorate with the exotic dried fruit and ginger.

For parkin, make the cake as above, replacing the wholemeal flour with 150 g (5 oz) medium oatmeal. Spoon into a greased and lined 20 cm (8 inch) square cake tin (see page 15) and bake at 150°C (300°F), Gas Mark 2, for 50–60 minutes or until firm to the touch. When cool, turn out, peel off the lining paper and wrap in greaseproof paper. Cut into 16 squares to serve.

apricot teabread

Cuts into **10**
Preparation time **25 minutes**, plus soaking
Cooking time **1 hour**

100 g (3½ oz) **ready-to-eat dried apricots**, chopped
100 g (3½ oz) **sultanas**
100 g (3½ oz) **raisins**
150 g (5 oz) **caster sugar**
300 ml (½ pint) **hot strong tea**
275 g (9 oz) **self-raising flour**
1 teaspoon **bicarbonate of soda**
1 teaspoon **ground cinnamon**
1 **egg**, beaten

Put the dried fruits and sugar in a bowl, add the hot tea and mix together. Leave to soak for 4 hours or overnight.

Mix together the flour, bicarbonate of soda and cinnamon, add to the soaked fruit with the egg and mix together well.

Spoon the mixture into a greased and lined 1 kg (2 lb) or 1.3 litre (2¼ pint) loaf tin (see page 15) and level the surface. Bake in the centre of a preheated oven, 160°C (325°F), Gas Mark 3, for about 1 hour until well risen, the top has cracked and a skewer inserted into the centre comes out clean.

Leave to cool in the tin for 10 minutes, then loosen at the ends and transfer to a wire rack. Peel off the lining paper and leave to cool completely. Cut into slices and spread with a little butter to serve.

For prune & orange bread, replace the apricots and sultanas with 175 g (6 oz) chopped stoned prunes, and increase the quantity of raisins to 125 g (4 oz). Mix with the caster sugar as above, add the grated rind of 1 orange, then soak in 150 ml (¼ pint) orange juice and 150 ml (¼ pint) boiling water instead of the tea. Add the flour, bicarbonate of soda and beaten egg as above, omitting the cinnamon. Spoon into the loaf tin and bake as above.

candied pistachio cake

Cuts into **8**
Preparation time **25 minutes**, plus cooling
Cooking time **55 minutes**

2 teaspoons **egg white**
150 g (5 oz) **shelled pistachio nuts**
2 tablespoons **vanilla sugar**
125 g (4 oz) **slightly salted butter**, softened
100 g (3½ oz) **caster sugar**
finely grated rind of 1 **lemon**
2 **eggs**, separated
75 g (3 oz) **plain flour**
½ teaspoon **baking powder**
sifted **icing sugar**, for dusting

Whisk the 2 teaspoons egg white in a bowl to break it up. Add the pistachio nuts and coat thinly in the egg white. Sprinkle in the vanilla sugar, turning the nuts to coat, then spread out on a baking sheet lined with baking parchment. Bake in a preheated oven, 160°C (325°F), Gas Mark 3, for 10 minutes. Leave to cool, then roughly chop.

Beat together the butter, 75 g (3 oz) of the caster sugar and the lemon rind in a bowl until very pale and fluffy. Beat in the egg yolks. Sift in the flour and baking powder, then stir in the nuts, reserving 3 tablespoons.

Whisk the egg whites in a clean bowl with a hand-held electric whisk until peaking. Gradually whisk in the remaining sugar, a spoonful at a time. Stir a third of the mixture into the creamed mixture using a large metal spoon. Gently stir in the remaining egg whites.

Spoon the mixture into a greased and lined 1 kg (2 lb) or 1.3 litre (2¼ pint) loaf tin (see page 15) and level the surface. Scatter with the reserved nuts and bake in the oven for about 45 minutes or until firm to the touch and a skewer inserted into the centre comes out clean. Loosen the cake at the ends and transfer to a wire rack to cool. Peel off the lining paper and dust with sifted icing sugar. Serve with Honeyed Yogurt Cream, if liked (see below).

For honeyed yogurt cream, to serve as an accompaniment, whip 100 ml (3½ fl oz) double cream in a bowl until thickened. Stir in 200 ml (7 fl oz) Greek yogurt and 4 tablespoons clear honey. Serve spooned over the cake and drizzle with extra honey, if liked.

beer & raisin slice

Cuts into **10**
Preparation time **15 minutes**, plus standing
Cooking time **55 minutes**

150 g (5 oz) **raisins**
300 ml (½ pint) **strong ale**
150 g (5 oz) **dark muscovado sugar**
1 teaspoon **caraway seeds** (optional)
1 **egg**, beaten
175 g (6 oz) **self-raising flour**
150 g (5 oz) **plain wholemeal flour**
1 teaspoon **baking powder**

Put the raisins and ale in a small saucepan and bring just to the boil. Pour into a large bowl and leave to stand until cold.

Stir the sugar, caraway seeds, if using, and egg into the beer mixture. Add the flours and baking powder and stir in.

Spoon the mixture into a greased and lined 1 kg (2 lb) or 1.3 litre (2¼ pint) loaf tin (see page 15) and spread into the corners. Bake in a preheated oven, 180°C (350°F), Gas Mark 4, for about 50 minutes until risen, firm to the touch and a skewer inserted into the centre comes out clean. Loosen the cake at the ends and transfer to a wire rack. Peel off the lining paper and leave to cool.

For chunky fruit & nut teabread, put 200 g (7 oz) mixed dried fruit and 175 ml (6 fl oz) cider or apple juice in a saucepan and bring to the boil. Pour into a bowl and leave to cool. Add 50 g (2 oz) ground almonds, 50 g (2 oz) roughly chopped walnuts, 100 g (3½ oz) caster sugar, 1 beaten egg, 75 g (3 oz) self-raising flour and ½ teaspoon baking powder and stir until combined. Spoon into a greased and lined 500 g (1 lb) or 750 ml (1¼ pint) loaf tin and bake as above.

rich chocolate teabread

Cuts into **10**
Preparation time **20 minutes**, plus cooling
Cooking time **1 hour 20 minutes**

50 g (2 oz) **cocoa powder**
200 ml (7 fl oz) **boiling water**
225 g (7½ oz) **plain dark chocolate**, diced
100 g (3½ oz) **slightly salted butter**, softened
250 g (8 oz) **light muscovado sugar**
2 **eggs**
175 g (6 oz) **plain flour**
½ teaspoon **bicarbonate of soda**
1 teaspoon **vanilla extract**

For the topping
75 g (3 oz) **plain dark chocolate**, chopped
2 tablespoons **golden syrup**
40 g (1½ oz) **butter**

Put the cocoa powder in a heatproof bowl and whisk in the measurement water. Tip in 125 g (4 oz) of the chocolate and leave to cool, stirring frequently to melt the chocolate.

Beat together the butter, sugar, eggs, flour, bicarbonate of soda and vanilla in a bowl until pale and creamy. Stir in the chocolate mixture and remaining diced chocolate.

Spoon the mixture into a greased and lined 1.25 kg (2½ lb) or 1.5 litre (2½ pint) loaf tin (see page 15) and level the surface. Bake in a preheated oven, 160°C (325°F), Gas Mark 3, for about 1¼ hours or until a skewer inserted into the centre comes out clean. Loosen the cake at the ends and transfer to a wire rack. Peel off the lining paper and leave to cool.

Make the topping. Put all the ingredients in a small saucepan and heat very gently until melted. Remove from the heat and leave until the chocolate has melted, stirring frequently. Leave to cool slightly, then spread over the cake.

For fresh ginger butter, to replace the topping and spread over the sliced cake, finely grate 50 g (2 oz) fresh root ginger, working over a bowl to catch all the juices. Press the juice and ginger pulp through a sieve into a clean bowl. Add 100 g (3½ oz) softened unsalted butter and 75 g (3 oz) sifted icing sugar and beat well until smooth and creamy.

cookies & bars

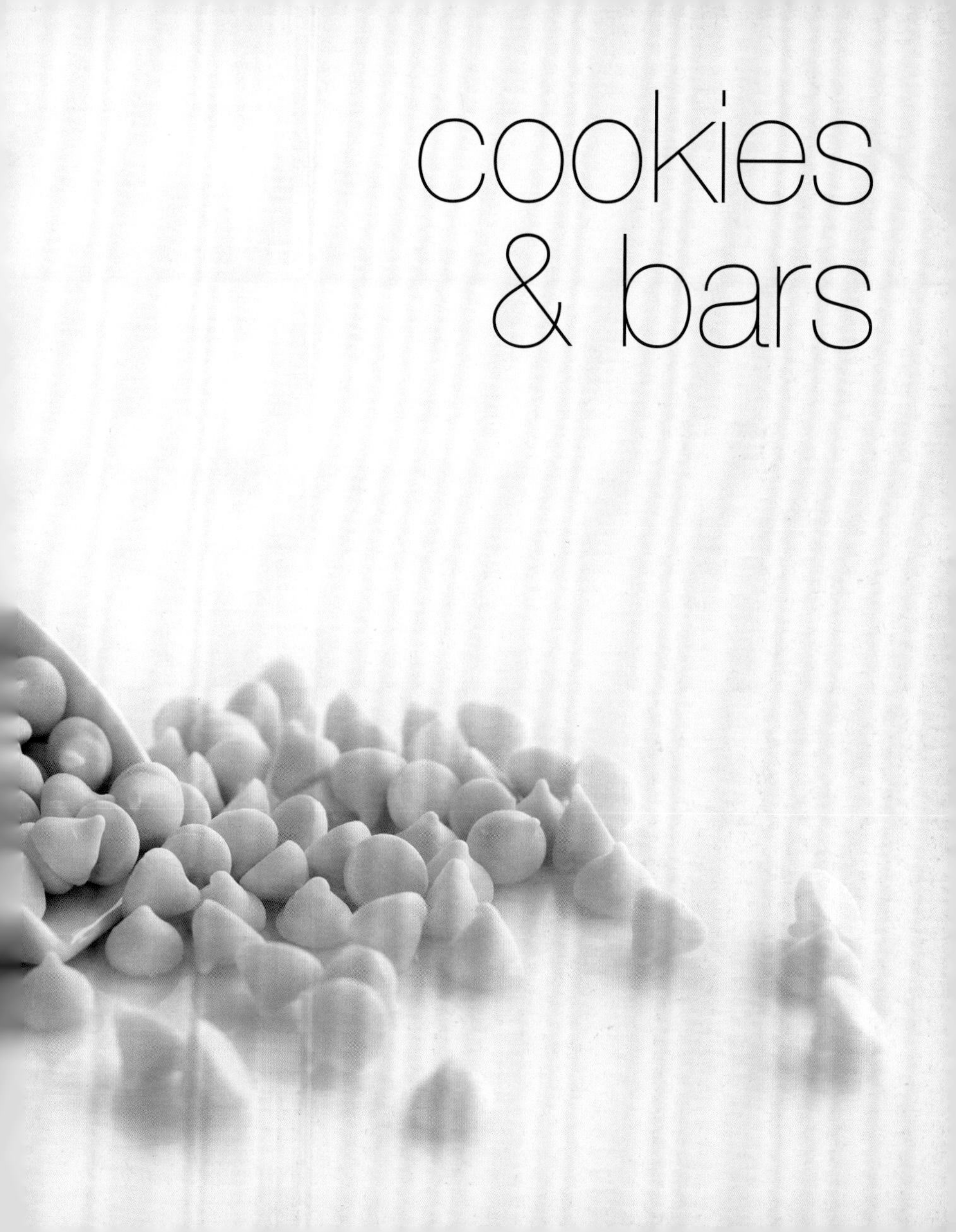

strawberry shortbreads

Makes about **12**
Preparation time **25 minutes**, plus chilling
Cooking time **15 minutes**

200 g (7 oz) **plain flour**
50 g (2 oz) **cornflour**
175 g (6 oz) **slightly salted butter**, chilled and diced
75 g (3 oz) **caster sugar**

For the filling
125 g (4 oz) **icing sugar**, sifted, plus extra for dusting
75 g (3 oz) **unsalted butter**, softened
1 teaspoon **vanilla extract**
1 teaspoon **boiling water**
5 tablespoons **strawberry jam**

Put the flours in a bowl or food processor. Add the butter and rub in with the fingertips or process until the mixture resembles coarse breadcrumbs. Add the sugar and mix or blend to a dough. Wrap in clingfilm and chill for 1 hour.

Roll out the dough on a lightly floured surface to 5 mm (¼ inch) thick. Cut out about 24 rounds using a 5 cm (2 inch) plain biscuit cutter, re-rolling the trimmings to make more. Place slightly apart on a large greased baking sheet and bake in a preheated oven, 190°C (375°F), Gas Mark 5, for 15 minutes until very pale golden. Transfer to a wire rack to cool.

Make the filling. Beat together the icing sugar, butter and vanilla in a bowl until smooth. Add the measurement water and beat until pale and creamy. Sandwich the biscuits together in pairs using the buttercream and jam. Serve dusted with sifted icing sugar.

For all-butter shortbread, put 150 g (5 oz) plain flour and 2 tablespoons rice flour in a food processor. Add 100 g (3½ oz) slightly salted butter, chilled and diced, and process until the mixture resembles breadcrumbs. Add 50 g (2 oz) caster sugar and blend to a dough. Press into a lightly greased 18 cm (7 inch) sandwich tin, pushing down firmly in an even layer. Prick all over with a fork. Bake in a preheated oven, 160°C (325°F), Gas Mark 3, for about 40 minutes or until pale golden. Mark into triangles, then sprinkle with caster sugar. Leave to cool in the tin for 10 minutes, then transfer to a wire rack to cool completely.

cardamom & orange biscuits

Makes about **12**
Preparation time **15 minutes**, plus chilling
Cooking time **15 minutes**

12 **cardamom pods**
150 g (5 oz) **plain flour**
100 g (3½ oz) **slightly salted butter**, chilled and diced
50 g (2 oz) **icing sugar**, sifted
1 **egg yolk**
finely grated rind of 1 **orange**

For the icing
75 g (3 oz) **icing sugar**, sifted
1 tablespoon **orange juice**

Crush the cardamom pods using a pestle and mortar or a small bowl and the end of a rolling pin. Discard the shells and crush the seeds as finely as possible.

Put the flour and crushed seeds in a bowl or food processor. Add the butter and rub in with the fingertips or process until the mixture resembles coarse breadcrumbs. Add the icing sugar and stir in or blend briefly. Add the egg yolk and orange rind and mix or blend to a dough. Wrap in clingfilm and chill for 1 hour.

Roll out the dough on a lightly floured surface to 5 mm (¼ inch) thick. Cut out about 12 heart shapes using a 5–6 cm (2–2½ inch) heart biscuit cutter, re-rolling the trimmings to make more. Place slightly apart on a large greased baking sheet and bake in a preheated oven, 190°C (375°F), Gas Mark 5, for about 15 minutes until pale golden. Transfer to a wire rack to cool.

Make the icing. Beat together the icing sugar and orange juice in a bowl to make a smooth, thin icing. Drizzle lines of icing over the biscuits to decorate.

For vanilla dessert biscuits, make and chill the dough as above, omitting the cardamom and replacing the orange rind with 1 teaspoon vanilla bean paste or extract. Roll out as above and cut out about 12 rounds using a 5–6 cm (2–2½ inch) plain biscuit cutter. Bake as above and serve lightly dusted with sifted icing sugar.

easy almond macaroons

Makes about **15**
Preparation time **10 minutes**
Cooking time **15 minutes**

2 **egg whites**
100 g (3½ oz) **golden caster sugar**
100 g (3½ oz) **ground almonds**
blanched almonds, to decorate

Whisk the egg whites in a clean bowl with a hand-held electric whisk until peaking. Gradually whisk in the sugar, a spoonful at a time, until thick and glossy. Add the ground almonds and stir in until combined.

Drop dessertspoonfuls of the mixture, slightly apart, on a large baking sheet lined with baking parchment. Press an almond on top of each.

Bake in a preheated oven, 180°C (350°F), Gas Mark 4, for about 15 minutes until the biscuits are pale golden and just crisp. Leave on the paper for 5 minutes, then transfer to a wire rack to cool.

For scribbled chocolate macaroons, make the macaroons as above, replacing 20 g (¾ oz) of the ground almonds with 20 g (¾ oz) cocoa powder and omitting the whole almonds. Melt 50 g (2 oz) plain dark or milk chocolate (see page 17), then drizzle over the cooled biscuits with a teaspoon.

mini orange shortbreads

Makes about **80**
Preparation time **10 minutes**
Cooking time **10–12 minutes**

250 g (8 oz) **plain flour**, sifted
175 g (6 oz) **slightly salted butter**, chilled and diced
grated rind of 1 **orange**
½ teaspoon **ground mixed spice**
75 g (3 oz) **caster sugar**
2 teaspoons **cold water**

To serve
2 teaspoons **icing sugar**
1 teaspoon **cocoa powder**

Put the flour in a bowl or food processor. Add the butter and rub in with the fingertips or process until the mixture resembles fine breadcrumbs. Add the remaining ingredients with the measurement water and mix or blend to a dough.

Roll out the dough on a lightly floured surface to 2.5 mm (⅛ inch) thick. Cut out about 80 rounds using a 1.5 cm (¾ inch) plain biscuit cutter, re-rolling the trimmings to make more. Place on 2 large baking sheets lined with baking parchment.

Bake in a preheated oven, 200°C (400°F), Gas Mark 6, for 10–12 minutes until golden. Transfer to a wire rack to cool.

Sift together the icing sugar and cocoa powder and dust a little over the shortbreads before serving.

For lemon & cardamom shortbreads, crush 10 cardamom pods using a pestle and mortar or a small bowl and the end of a rolling pin. Discard the husks and crush the seeds a little more until ground. Make the shortbreads as above, replacing the orange rind and mixed spice with the finely grated rind of 1 lemon and the ground cardamom, and the cold water with 2 teaspoons lemon juice. Serve dusted with sifted icing sugar.

almond biscuits

Makes about **14**
Preparation time **20 minutes**
Cooking time **10 minutes**

150 g (5 oz) **ground almonds**
1 tablespoon **plain flour**
175 g (6 oz) **caster sugar,** plus extra for coating
½ teaspoon **baking powder**
1 egg white
½ teaspoon **vanilla extract**

Mix together the ground almonds, flour, sugar and baking powder in a large bowl. Whisk the egg white in a separate clean bowl until it holds its shape. Fold into the almond mixture. Add the vanilla and mix to a dough.

Dust a work surface with caster sugar. Shape 1 tablespoon of the dough into a sausage about 6 cm (2½ inches) long, then roll in the sugar. Place on a baking sheet lined with baking parchment. Repeat with the remaining dough, spacing them well apart on the baking sheet.

Bake in a preheated oven, 200°C (400°F), Gas Mark 6, for 10 minutes until lightly golden. Transfer to a wire rack to cool.

For candied peel & sultana biscuits, make the biscuits as above, reducing the caster sugar to 150 g (5 oz) and stirring in 2 tablespoons chopped candied peel, and adding 2 tablespoons sultanas with the vanilla extract.

pistachio biscotti

Makes about **24**
Preparation time **15 minutes**, plus cooling
Cooking time **30 minutes**

25 g (1 oz) **slightly salted butter**, softened
50 g (2 oz) **caster sugar**
finely grated rind of 1 **lemon**
125 g (4 oz) **self-raising flour**
½ teaspoon **baking powder**
1 egg yolk
1 tablespoon **egg white**
65 g (2½ oz) **shelled pistachio nut**s, skinned and roughly chopped

Beat together the butter, sugar and lemon rind in a bowl until pale and fluffy. Sift in the flour and baking powder, then add the egg yolk, egg white and pistachios and mix to a soft dough.

Divide the dough into 2 pieces and shape each into a sausage about 15 cm (6 inches) long. Place the pieces, well spaced apart, on a greased baking sheet and flatten each to a depth of 1 cm (½ inch).

Bake in a preheated oven, 160°C (325°F), Gas Mark 3, for 20 minutes until risen and turning pale golden. Remove from the oven and leave to cool for 10 minutes, leaving the oven on. Using a serrated knife, cut the biscuits across into 1 cm (½ inch) thick slices. Return to the baking sheet, cut sides face up, and bake for a further 10 minutes to crisp up. Transfer to a wire rack to cool.

For walnut oat cookies, mix together 50 g (2 oz) sifted self-raising flour, 50 g (2 oz) porridge oats, 40 g (1½ oz) chopped walnuts and ¼ teaspoon bicarbonate of soda in a bowl. Put 50 g (2 oz) slightly salted butter, 50 g (2 oz) golden caster sugar and 1 tablespoon golden syrup in a small saucepan. Heat gently until the butter has melted. Add to the oat mixture and stir well to mix. Roll teaspoonfuls of the mixture into small balls and space well apart on a greased baking sheet. Bake as above for about 15 minutes until pale golden. Transfer to a wire rack to cool.

chunky monkeys

Makes **12**
Preparation time **10 minutes**
Cooking time **10–12 minutes**

200 g (7 oz) **plain flour**
1 teaspoon b**icarbonate of soda**
125 g (4 oz) **caster sugar**
125 g (4 oz) **butter**, chilled and diced
1 **egg**
1 tablespoon **milk**
150 g (5 oz) **white chocolate**, roughly chopped
75 g (3 oz) **natural glacé cherries**, roughly chopped

Mix together the flour, bicarbonate of soda and sugar in a bowl. Add the butter and rub in with the fingertips until the mixture resembles breadcrumbs.

Beat together the egg and milk in a separate bowl. Add the chopped chocolate and glacé cherries, then mix into the flour mixture and stir well until smooth.

Drop heaped tablespoonfuls of the mixture, well spaced apart, on to a greased baking sheet and bake in a preheated oven, 180°C (350°F), Gas Mark 4, for 10–12 minutes until lightly golden. Leave to harden on the sheet for 2 minutes, then transfer to a wire rack to cool.

For double chocolate chunky monkeys, make the biscuits as above, replacing 15 g (½ oz) of the flour with 15 g (½ oz) cocoa powder and the cherries with 75 g (3 oz) toasted blanched hazelnuts, roughly chopped.

chocolate chip cookies

Makes **16**
Preparation time **10 minutes**
Cooking time **15 minutes**

125 g (4 oz) **unsalted butter**, softened
175 g (6 oz) **soft light brown sugar**
1 teaspoon **vanilla extract**
1 **egg**, lightly beaten
1 tablespoon **milk**
200 g (7 oz) **plain flour**
1 teaspoon **baking powder**
250 g (8 oz) **plain dark chocolate chips**

Beat together the butter and sugar in a large bowl until pale and fluffy. Mix in the vanilla, then gradually beat in the egg, beating well after each addition. Stir in the milk. Sift in the flour and baking powder, then fold in. Stir in the chocolate chips.

Drop level tablespoonfuls of the mixture, about 3.5 cm (1½ inches) apart, on to a large baking sheet lined with baking parchment, then lightly press with a floured fork. Bake in a preheated oven, 180°C (350°F), Gas Mark 4, for 15 minutes or until lightly golden. Transfer to a wire rack to cool.

For chocolate & mandarin log, make the biscuits as above and leave to cool completely. Drain a 300 g (10 oz) can mandarin segments and finely chop, reserving a few whole segments for decoration. Whip 300 ml (½ pint) double cream and 25 g (1 oz) sifted icing sugar in a bowl until thick, then fold in the chopped mandarins. Sandwich the cookies one on top of the other with half the mandarin cream, then carefully set the log on its side and wrap in foil. Chill for at least 2–3 hours or overnight. Just before serving, put the log on a serving plate, cover with the remaining mandarin cream and decorate with the reserved mandarins. Serve in slices, cut on the diagonal.

chunky white chocolate cookies

Makes about **20**
Preparation time **20 minutes**
Cooking time **15 minutes**

50 g (2 oz) **slightly salted butter**, softened
125 g (4 oz) **light muscovado sugar**
1 **egg**, beaten
150 g (5 oz) **self-raising flour**
150 g (5 oz) **white chocolate chips** or **white chocolate**, chopped

Beat together the butter and sugar in a bowl until combined. Beat in the egg until smooth and creamy. Add the flour and chocolate to the bowl and mix to a paste.

Roll heaped teaspoonfuls of the mixture into balls and place, well spaced apart, on 2 greased baking sheets.

Bake in a preheated oven, 180°C (350°F), Gas Mark 4, for about 15 minutes or until the cookies have spread and are pale golden. Leave to harden on the sheets for 2 minutes, then transfer to a wire rack to cool.

For chocolate sandwich cookies, make the dough as above, omitting the chocolate chips and replacing 25 g (1 oz) of the flour with 25 g (1 oz) cocoa powder. Shape into small balls, about 2.5 cm (1 inch) in diameter, and bake as above. Melt 75 g (3 oz) milk chocolate (see page 17), then stir in 5 g (¼ oz) butter until melted. Use to sandwich the cooled cookies together.

peanut butter cookies

Makes **18–20**
Preparation time **15 minutes**
Cooking time **18–20 minutes**

75 g (3 oz) **crunchy peanut butter**
100 g (3½ oz) **golden caster sugar**
50 g (2 oz) **slightly salted butter**, softened
1 **egg**, beaten
100 g (3½ oz) **self-raising flour**
40 g (1½ oz) **salted peanuts**, chopped

Beat together the peanut butter, sugar and butter in a bowl until well combined. Add the egg and flour and mix to a paste.

Roll teaspoonfuls of the mixture into small walnut-sized balls, then place slightly apart on a large greased baking sheet and flatten with a fork. Scatter the chopped peanuts over the cookies.

Bake in a preheated oven, 180°C (350°F), Gas Mark 4, for 18–20 minutes until risen and deep golden. Transfer to a wire rack to cool.

For peanut thumbprint cookies, make the dough as above, adding an extra 50 g (2 oz) flour and 50 g (2 oz) finely chopped salted peanuts to the dough. Shape the mixture into a log on a floured surface and cut into 20 even-sized pieces. Roll each into a ball and flatten slightly on the baking sheet. Push a hole into the centre of each with your floured thumb. Bake as above and transfer to a wire rack to cool. Spoon ½ teaspoon raspberry or strawberry jam into the centre of each.

sultana & lemon flapjacks

Cuts into **12**
Preparation time **10 minutes**
Cooking time **20 minutes**

175 g (6 oz) **unsalted butter**
50 g (2 oz) **caster sugar**
150 g (5 oz) **golden syrup**
finely grated rind of 2 **lemons**
250 g (8 oz) **porridge oats**
75 g (3 oz) **sultanas**

Put the butter, sugar, golden syrup and lemon rind in a saucepan and heat gently until the butter has melted. Remove from the heat and stir in the oats and sultanas. Mix well.

Spoon the mixture into a greased and parchment-lined 20 cm (8 inch) square shallow baking tin (see page 15) and level the surface with the back of a spoon.

Bake in a preheated oven, 180°C (350°F), Gas Mark 4, for about 20 minutes until turning golden. Leave to cool in the tin for 10 minutes, then transfer to a wire rack to cool completely. Peel off the lining paper and cut into squares or fingers.

For chewy breakfast bars, mix together 65 g (2½ oz) porridge oats, 200 g (7 oz) mixed chopped nuts, 50 g (2 oz) ground almonds, 100 g (3½ oz) chopped stoned dates, 100 g (3½ oz) chopped dried figs, 50 g (2 oz) sultanas or raisins and 3 tablespoons pumpkin seeds. Add 100 ml (3½ fl oz) clear honey or agave nectar and mix well until the ingredients start to bind together. Pack into the tin, pressing down firmly with the back of a dampened spoon. Bake as above. Once cooled, cut into 12 fingers or squares.

chocolate refrigerator cake

Cuts into **30**
Preparation time **15 minutes**, plus chilling
Cooking time **5 minutes**

- 500 g (1 lb) **plain dark chocolate**, broken into pieces
- 125 g (4 oz) **unsalted butter**
- 100 g (3½ oz) **digestive biscuits**, roughly crushed
- 100 g (3½ oz) **dried figs**, roughly chopped
- 50 g (2 oz) **dried cranberries**
- 50 g (2 oz) **blanched hazelnuts**, toasted
- 50 g (2 oz) **blanched almonds**, toasted and roughly chopped
- sifted **icing sugar**, for dusting (optional)

Melt the chocolate and butter in a heatproof bowl set over a saucepan of gently simmering water (don't let the base of the bowl touch the water), then stir in the remaining ingredients.

Spoon the mixture into a 23 x 18 cm (9 x 7 inch) shallow baking tin, greased and base-lined with baking parchment (see page 15). Press well into the base and sides of the tin and smooth the surface.

Cover with foil and chill for 4 hours or overnight. Loosen the edges of the cake and turn out on to a board. Peel off the lining paper, cut into thin fingers and serve dusted with sifted icing sugar, if liked.

For white chocolate rocky road cake, melt 375 g (12 oz) white chocolate, broken into pieces (see page 17). Meanwhile, grease a 1 kg (2 lb) loaf tin and line with baking parchment (see page 15). Stir 200 g (7 oz) roughly chopped Turkish delight (any flavour of your choice), 75 g (3 oz) shelled pistachio nuts and 25 g (1 oz) desiccated coconut into the melted chocolate. Pour the mixture into the prepared tin, smooth the surface and chill for 4 hours. Turn out, peel off the lining paper and cut into slices.

marshmallow crackle squares

Cuts into **14**
Preparation time **10 minutes**, plus setting
Cooking time **5 minutes**

200 g (7 oz) **marshmallows**, halved
40 g (1½ oz) **unsalted butter**, diced
100 g (3½ oz) **crisped rice cereal**
pink sugar sprinkles, to decorate

Reserve 50 g (2 oz) of the white marshmallows. Put 25 g (1 oz) of the butter and the remaining marshmallows into a saucepan and heat very gently until melted. Remove from the heat and stir in the cereal until evenly coated.

Spoon the mixture into an 18 cm (7 inch) square shallow baking tin, greased and lined with baking parchment (see page 15), and pack down firmly with the back of a lightly oiled spoon.

Place the remaining butter and reserved marshmallows in a small saucepan and heat gently until melted. Drizzle into the tin in lines, then scatter the sprinkles over the top. Leave in a cool place for 2 hours or until firm.

Turn out of the tin on to a board, peel off the lining paper and cut into small squares.

For chocolate crackle cakes, melt 100 g (3½ oz) milk chocolate, broken into pieces, and 1 tablespoon golden syrup in a heatproof bowl set over a saucepan of gently simmering water (don't let the base of the bowl touch the water). Put 100 g (3½ oz) cornflakes in a plastic bag and crush lightly using a rolling pin. Tip into the chocolate mixture and stir well until thoroughly combined. Pack into 14–16 small paper cupcake cases and top with chocolate sprinkles. Leave to set for at least 1 hour before serving.

date & sesame bars

Cuts into **16**
Preparation time **15 minutes**
Cooking time **25–30 minutes**

125 g (4 oz) **unsalted butter**, diced
75 g (3 oz) **golden caster sugar**
1 tablespoon **clear honey**
150 g (5 oz) **stoned dates**, chopped
125 g (4 oz) **self-raising flour**
125 g (4 oz) **medium oatmeal**
50 g (2 oz) **sesame seeds**

Put the butter, sugar and honey in a saucepan and heat gently until the butter has melted, then remove from the heat and stir in the dates.

Place the flour and oatmeal in a bowl. Add the sesame seeds, reserving 2 tablespoons, pour in the butter mixture and mix until combined.

Spoon into a greased 28 x 18 cm (11 x 7 inch) shallow baking tin and level the surface. Scatter with the reserved seeds. Bake in a preheated oven, 180°C (350°F), Gas Mark 4, for 20–25 minutes or until pale golden and firm to the touch. Leave to cool in the tin, then turn out on to a board and cut into bars.

For sticky cereal bars, put 75 g (3 oz) unsalted butter and 4 tablespoons golden syrup in a saucepan and heat until melted. Remove from the heat and add 125 g (4 oz) porridge oats, 25 g (1 oz) desiccated coconut, 75 g (3 oz) dried cranberries or blueberries and 25 g (1 oz) golden caster sugar. Tip into a greased and lined 1 kg (2 lb) loaf tin (see page 15) and level the surface. Bake in a preheated oven, 190°C (375°F), Gas Mark 5, for about 15 minutes or until turning deep golden around the edges. Leave to cool in the tin, then turn out, peel off the lining paper and cut into bars.

blueberry & oat bars

Cuts into **12**
Preparation time **20 minutes**
Cooking time **50–60 minutes**

100 g (3½ oz) **plain wholemeal flour**
75 g (3 oz) **self-raising flour**
175 g (6 oz) **slightly salted butter**, chilled and diced
½ teaspoon **ground cinnamon**
175 g (6 oz) **porridge oats**
150 g (5 oz) **light muscovado sugar**
200 g (7 oz) **fresh blueberries**
vanilla sugar, for sprinkling

Put the flours in a bowl or food processor. Add the butter and rub in with the fingertips or process until the mixture resembles breadcrumbs. Add the cinnamon, oats and muscovado sugar and stir in or blend briefly until the mixture makes coarse crumbs and starts to cling together.

Tip about half the mixture into a greased 28 x 18 cm (11 x 7 inch) shallow baking tin and spread in an even layer. Pack down with the back of a spoon to make a firm base. Scatter with the blueberries and sprinkle with the remaining crumble mixture.

Bake in a preheated oven, 180°C (350°F), Gas Mark 4, for about 50–60 minutes until the crumble is deep golden. Leave to cool in the tin, then sprinkle with vanilla sugar and cut into bars.

For oat & seed cookies, put 125 g (4 oz) self-raising flour, 125 g (4 oz) porridge oats, 50 g (2 oz) sunflower seeds and ½ teaspoon bicarbonate of soda into a bowl. Put 125 g (4 oz) unsalted butter, 125 g (4 oz) golden caster sugar and 2 tablespoons golden syrup in a saucepan and heat until the butter has melted. Add to the flour mixture and beat well to mix. Roll heaped teaspoonfuls of the mixture into balls and place, spaced well apart, on greased baking sheets. Bake in a preheated oven, 180°C (350°F), Gas Mark 4, for about 18 minutes until risen and golden. Leave to cool on the baking sheets for 5 minutes, then transfer to a wire rack to cool.

hazelnut & polenta wedges

Cuts into **8**
Preparation time **10 minutes**
Cooking time **35 minutes**

150 g (5 oz) **blanched hazelnuts**
150 g (5 oz) **polenta**
125 g (4 oz) **caster sugar**
100 g (3½ oz) **slightly salted butter**, softened
50 g (2 oz) **icing sugar**, sifted

Put the hazelnuts in a food processor and process until fairly finely chopped. Scoop out 3 tablespoons of the hazelnuts, then whizz the nuts in the processor until the consistency of ground almonds. Add the polenta, caster sugar and butter and blend to a paste.

Pack into a greased and base-lined 18 cm (7 inch) sandwich tin (see page 13) and press down in an even layer with your fingers. Sprinkle with the reserved hazelnuts. Bake in a preheated oven, 190°C (375°F), Gas Mark 5, for 35 minutes or until risen, pale golden and still very soft. Leave to cool in the tin.

Beat together the icing sugar and a dash of water in a bowl to make a smooth, spoonable icing, then drizzle over the biscuit and cut into wedges.

For hazelnut slice with peaches & cream, make the biscuit as above, then leave to cool. Whip 150 ml (¼ pint) double cream, 2 tablespoons sifted icing sugar and 1 teaspoon vanilla extract in a bowl until just peaking. Halve, stone and thinly slice 1 ripe peach. Stir into the cream mixture and spoon over the top of the biscuit. Thinly slice another peach and scatter over the top along with a sprinkling of fresh redcurrants. Serve dusted with sifted icing sugar.

layered nutty bars

Cuts into **10 slices**
Preparation time **20 minutes**, plus chilling
Cooking time **5 minutes**

50 g (2 oz) **butter**
400 g (13 oz) **fat-free sweetened condensed milk**
200 g (7 oz) **plain dark chocolate**, broken into pieces
125 g (4 oz) **rich tea biscuits**
50 g (2 oz) **blanched hazelnuts**
100 g (3½ oz) **shelled pistachio nuts**

Put the butter, condensed milk and chocolate in a saucepan and heat gently for 3–4 minutes, stirring, until melted. Remove from the heat.

Place the biscuits in a plastic bag and crush roughly into chunky pieces using a rolling pin. Toast the hazelnuts under a preheated hot grill until lightly browned, then roughly chop with the pistachios.

Stir the biscuits into the chocolate mixture, then spoon half the mixture into a greased 20 cm (8 inch) spring-form cake tin and spread level. Reserve 2 tablespoons of the nuts for the top, then sprinkle the rest over the chocolate biscuit layer. Cover with the remaining chocolate mixture, level the surface and sprinkle with the reserved nuts.

Chill for 3–4 hours until firm, then loosen the edges and remove the ring and base. Cut into thin slices, or into tiny bite-sized pieces to make petits fours.

For gingered fruit bars, make the recipe as above, replacing the rich tea biscuits with 125 g (4 oz) digestive biscuits and the nuts with 50 g (2 oz) roughly chopped ready-to-eat dried apricots and 2 tablespoons chopped glacé ginger, reserving 2–3 tablespoons for the top.

candied pecan twists

Makes **24**
Preparation time **15 minutes**, plus cooling
Cooking time **25 minutes**

1 teaspoon **egg white**
50 g (2 oz) **pecan nuts**
1 tablespoon **vanilla sugar**
5 tablespoons **golden caster sugar**
375 g (12 oz) **ready-made puff pastry**
plain flour, for dusting

Whisk the egg white in a bowl to break it up. Add the pecans and coat thinly in the egg white. Sprinkle in the vanilla sugar, turning the nuts to coat, then spread out on a baking sheet lined with baking parchment. Bake in a preheated oven, 160°C (325°F), Gas Mark 3, for about 5 minutes until beginning to colour. Leave to cool, then finely chop. Increase the oven temperature to 220°C (425°F), Gas Mark 7.

Sprinkle 1 tablespoon of the caster sugar on the work surface. Roll out the pastry on the surface to a 25 x 15 cm (10 x 6 inch) rectangle. Sprinkle the pastry with another tablespoon of the sugar and roll in gently. Halve the pastry and place one piece on top of the other. Flatten slightly with the rolling pin and sprinkle with another tablespoon of the sugar and the chopped nuts. Roll out again to a 24 cm (9 inch) square, lightly flouring the work surface if the mixture is sticky. Sprinkle with another tablespoon of the sugar and roll gently.

Trim the edges, cut in half, then cut each half across into 2 cm (¾ inch) wide strips. Twist each strip several times and place slightly apart on a large baking sheet lined with baking parchment. Sprinkle the remaining sugar along each twist. Bake for about 20 minutes until puffed and golden. Transfer to a wire rack to cool. Serve with Vanilla Cheesecake Dip, if liked (see below).

For vanilla cheesecake dip, to serve as an accompaniment, beat 200 g (7 oz) mascarpone cheese in a bowl to soften, then beat in 1 teaspoon vanilla bean paste or extract, 2 tablespoons caster sugar and 4 tablespoons single cream. Cover and chill until ready to serve.

Prestige

traybakes & brownies

iced fig slice

Cuts into **12**
Preparation time **25 minutes**
Cooking time **1 hour**

225 g (7½ oz) **ready-made puff pastry**
175 g (6 oz) **slightly salted butter**, softened
175 g (6 oz) **caster sugar**
200 g (7 oz) **self-raising flour**
½ teaspoon **baking powder**
3 **eggs**
6 **figs**, quartered

For the icing
100 g (3½ oz) **icing sugar**, sifted
1 tablespoon **lemon juice**

Roll out the pastry on a lightly floured surface and use to line a greased 23 cm (9 inch) square shallow baking tin or small roasting tin. Line the pastry case with greaseproof paper and fill with baking beans (or dried beans reserved for the purpose). Bake in a preheated oven, 200°C (400°F), Gas Mark 6, for 15 minutes. Remove from the oven and remove the paper and beans. Reduce the oven temperature to 180°C (350°F), Gas Mark 4.

Beat together the butter, sugar, flour, baking powder and eggs in a bowl until pale and creamy. Spoon over the pastry base and level the surface. Arrange the figs over the top. Bake in the oven for about 45 minutes or until risen and golden. Leave to cool in the tin.

Make the icing. Beat together the icing sugar and lemon juice in a bowl to make a smooth, spoonable icing. If necessary, beat in a dash of water or extra lemon juice. Drizzle the icing over the cake, then cut into squares or fingers.

For wholemeal pear & cardamom slice, make and bake the pastry case as above. Crush 15 cardamom pods using a pestle and mortar or a small bowl and the end of a rolling pin. Discard the husks and crush the seeds a little more. Make the sponge mixture as above, replacing the white flour with 200 g (7 oz) self-raising wholemeal flour and adding the ground seeds. Continue as above, replacing the figs with 4 cored and thickly sliced ripe pears.

sticky gingerbread

Cuts into **12**
Preparation time **20 minutes**
Cooking time **40 minutes**

225 g (7½ oz) **plain flour**
1 teaspoon **bicarbonate of soda**
2 teaspoons **ground ginger**
75 g (3 oz) **slightly salted butter**
125 g (4 oz) **light muscovado sugar**
75 g (3 oz) **golden syrup**
75 g (3 oz) **black treacle**
125 ml (4 fl oz) **buttermilk**
1 **egg**, beaten
75 g (3 oz) **sultanas**

For the glaze
3 tablespoons **ginger marmalade** or **jam**
1 teaspoon **water**

Put the flour, bicarbonate of soda and ginger into a bowl. Put the butter, sugar, golden syrup and treacle into a saucepan and heat gently without boiling until the butter has melted. Remove from the heat and stir in the buttermilk, then beat in the egg. Add to the dry ingredients with the sultanas and beat well to mix.

Spoon the mixture into a greased and lined 20 cm (8 inch) square cake tin or shallow baking tin (see page 15), spreading the mixture into the corners. Bake in a preheated oven, 160°C (325°F), Gas Mark 3, for about 30 minutes or until risen, just firm to the touch and a skewer inserted into the centre comes out clean. Leave to cool in the tin (the cake might sink slightly in the centre), then transfer to a board and peel off the lining paper.

Make the glaze. Put the marmalade or jam and measurement water in a small saucepan and heat gently. Press through a sieve to remove any lumps and brush over the gingerbread, then cut into bars.

For iced gingerbread, make the gingerbread as above. For the icing, finely grate 1 piece of stem ginger in syrup into a bowl. Add 75 g (3 oz) softened unsalted butter and 125 g (4 oz) sifted golden icing sugar and beat well, then add 2 teaspoons boiling water and beat until pale and creamy. Spread over the cooled cake, then cut into squares.

blueberry bakewell

Cuts into **18**
Preparation time **20 minutes**
Cooking time **1 hour**

350 g (11½ oz) **ready-made sweet shortcrust pastry**
6 tablespoons **blueberry jam** (see below for homemade)
125 g (4 oz) **slightly salted butter**, softened
125 g (4 oz) **caster sugar**
2 **eggs**
125 g (4 oz) **self-raising flour**
½ teaspoon **baking powder**
1 teaspoon **almond extract**
100 g (3½ oz) **ground almonds**
4 tablespoons **flaked almonds**
75 g (3 oz) **icing sugar**, sifted

Roll out the pastry on a lightly floured surface and use to line a greased 28 x 18 cm (11 x 7 inch) shallow baking tin. Line the pastry case with baking parchment and baking beans (or dried beans reserved for the purpose). Bake in a preheated oven, 200°C (400°F), Gas Mark 4, for 15 minutes. Remove the paper and beans and bake for a further 5 minutes. Reduce the oven temperature to 180°C (35°F), Gas Mark 4.

Spread the base of the pastry with the jam. Beat together the butter, caster sugar, eggs, flour, baking powder and almond extract in a bowl until smooth and creamy. Beat in the ground almonds. Spoon the mixture over the jam and spread gently in an even layer.

Scatter with the flaked almonds and bake in the oven for about 40 minutes until risen and just firm to the touch. Leave to cool in the tin.

Beat the icing sugar with a dash of water in a bowl to give the consistency of thin cream. Spread in a thin layer over the cake. Allow to set, then cut into squares or fingers.

For homemade blueberry jam, put 500 g (1 lb) fresh blueberries, 4 tablespoons lemon juice and 2 tablespoons water in a large saucepan and cook gently for about 8–10 minutes until the berries are soft. Stir in 450 g (14½ oz) preserving or granulated sugar and heat gently until the sugar dissolves. Bring to the boil and boil for 10–15 minutes until setting point is reached. Ladle into sterilized jars, cover and label.

cherry crumble cake

Cuts into **16**
Preparation time **25 minutes**, plus cooling
Cooking time **1 hour 5 minutes**

2 x 425 g (14 oz) cans **pitted black** or **red cherries**
2 teaspoons **cornflour**
250 g (8 oz) **self-raising flour**
1 teaspoon **ground mixed spice**
175 g (6 oz) **slightly salted butter**, chilled and diced
175 g (6 oz) **golden caster sugar**
50 g (2 oz) **ground almonds**
1 **egg**

Drain the cherries, reserving 7 tablespoons of the juice. Put a little of the reserved juice in a small saucepan with the cornflour and blend until smooth. Add the remaining juice and bring to the boil, stirring. Add the cherries and cook, stirring, for about 1 minute or until thickened slightly. Leave to cool.

Put the flour and mixed spice in a bowl or food processor. Add the butter and rub in with fingertips or process until the mixture resembles breadcrumbs. Add the sugar and ground almonds and mix or blend again until the mixture resembles a coarse crumble. Reserve 200 g (7 oz) of the mixture. Add the egg to the remaining mixture and mix to a soft dough.

Turn the dough into a greased 22–23 cm (8½–9 inch) square shallow baking tin and press it into the corners and slightly up the sides. Spread over the cherries to 1.5 cm (¾ inch) from the edges, then sprinkle with the reserved crumble mixture.

Bake in a preheated oven, 180°C (350°F), Gas Mark 4, for about 1 hour until the crumble is golden. Leave to cool in the tin, then cut into squares.

For apricot crumble cake, put 225 g (7½ oz) roughly chopped ready-to-eat dried apricots, 150 ml (¼ pint) apple or orange juice and 1½ teaspoons ground ginger in a saucepan. Bring to the boil, then reduce the heat and cook very gently for 5 minutes. Blend 1½ teaspoons cornflour with 2 tablespoons water and add to the pan. Cook, stirring, for 2 minutes until thickened slightly. Leave to cool. Make the cake as above, omitting the mixed spice and using the apricot mixture instead of the cherries.

sticky fig & banana traybake

Cuts into **6**
Preparation time **10 minutes**
Cooking time **20 minutes**

- 125 g (4 oz) **slightly salted butter**, softened
- 125 g (4 oz) **soft light brown sugar**
- 1 teaspoon **ground ginger**
- 2 **eggs**
- 125 g (4 oz) **plain flour**
- 3 **figs**, quartered
- 1 large **banana**, cut into chunks
- 2 tablespoons **maple syrup**

Beat together the butter and sugar in a bowl until smooth and creamy. Add the ginger, eggs and flour and beat again until smooth.

Spoon the mixture into a lightly greased 23 cm (9 inch) square shallow baking tin or ovenproof dish and level the surface. Toss the figs and banana with the maple syrup and arrange over the top, pressing the fruit into the cake in places.

Bake in a preheated oven, 180°C (350°F), Gas Mark 4, for 20 minutes until the cake is well risen and golden and the fruit is soft. Cut into squares and serve with scoops of ice cream or Vanilla Custard (see below).

For vanilla custard, to serve as an accompaniment, put 300 ml (½ pint) milk and the seeds of ½ vanilla pod in a saucepan and heat until boiling. Meanwhile, blend 2 egg yolks with 1 teaspoon cornflour and 2 tablespoons caster sugar in a heatproof bowl. Pour the boiled milk over the egg mixture and whisk well to blend. Return to the heat, stirring continuously until just beginning to boil and thicken. It will coat the back of a spoon.

sultana & pineapple slab cake

Cuts into **14**
Preparation time **15 minutes**, plus standing
Cooking time **45–50 minutes**

250 g (8 oz) **slightly salted butter**
150 g (5 oz) **golden syrup**
75 g (3 oz) **caster sugar**
100 g (3½ oz) **dried pineapple**, chopped
150 g (5 oz) **sultanas**
2 teaspoons **ground mixed spice**
½ teaspoon **bicarbonate of soda**
150 g (5 oz) **self-raising flour**
125 g (4 oz) **plain flour**
2 **eggs**, beaten
175 ml (6 fl oz) **soured cream**

For the frosting
250 g (8 oz) **mascarpone cheese**
50 g (2 oz) **unsalted butter,** softened
75 g (3 oz) **icing sugar**, sifted
2 teaspoons **lemon juice**

Put the butter, golden syrup and sugar in a saucepan and heat gently until the butter has melted. Remove from the heat and stir in the pineapple, sultanas and mixed spice. Leave to stand for 10 minutes, then stir in the bicarbonate of soda.

Place the flours in a large bowl. Stir together the eggs and soured cream, then add to the butter mixture and beat well to mix. Pour into the dry ingredients and stir well to mix.

Turn the mixture into a greased and lined 28 x 24 cm (11 x 9¼ inch) shallow baking tin or roasting tin (see page 15) and spread into the corners. Bake in a preheated oven, 180°C (350°F), Gas Mark 4, for about 40–45 minutes until just firm to the touch and a skewer inserted into the centre comes out clean. Leave to cool in the tin, then transfer to a board and peel off the lining paper.

Make the frosting. Beat together the mascarpone cheese and butter in a bowl until smooth. Stir in the icing sugar and lemon juice. Spread over the top of the cake, then cut into squares.

For chocolate slab cake, make the cake as above, omitting the pineapple, sultanas and mixed spice and replacing 50 g (2 oz) of the plain flour with 50 g (2 oz) cocoa powder. For chocolate buttercream, beat together 75 g (3 oz) softened unsalted butter and 125 g (4 oz) sifted golden icing sugar in a bowl until smooth. Beat in 75 g (3 oz) melted plain dark chocolate (see page 17). Spread over the top of the cake and scatter with chocolate sprinkles. Cut into squares.

easy cherry & almond traybake

Cuts into **12**
Preparation time **20 minutes**
Cooking time **25–30 minutes**

225 g (7½ oz) **self-raising flour**
1 teaspoon **baking powder**
100 g (3½ oz) **slightly salted butter**, chilled and diced
100 g (3½ oz) **golden caster sugar**
1 **egg**, beaten
125 ml (4 fl oz) **milk**
1 teaspoon **almond extract**
200 g (7 oz) **natural glacé cherries**, halved
50 g (2 oz) **flaked almonds**
sifted **icing sugar**, for dusting

Put the flour and baking powder in a bowl or food processor. Add the butter and rub in with the fingertips or process until the mixture resembles breadcrumbs. Add the caster sugar and stir in, or blend again, then tip into a bowl.

Mix together the egg, milk and almond extract in a jug. Add to the crumble mixture with half of the cherries and stir until evenly combined.

Spoon the mixture into a greased and lined 23 cm (9 inch) square shallow baking tin or small roasting tin (see page 15) and spread in an even layer. Scatter with the remaining cherries, then the flaked almonds.

Bake in a preheated oven, 180°C (350°F), Gas Mark 4, for 25–30 minutes or until golden and just firm to the touch. Leave to cool in the tin, then transfer to a board and peel off the lining paper. Dust with sifted icing sugar and cut into squares.

For redcurrant cream slices, make the cake as above, replacing the almond extract with 1 teaspoon vanilla bean paste or extract and omitting the glacé cherries. Cut the cooled cake into 12 squares, then halve each square horizontally. Remove any stalks from 150 g (5 oz) fresh redcurrants by running them between the tines of a fork. Whip 150 ml (¼ pint) double cream and 1 tablespoon sifted icing sugar in a bowl until peaking. Sandwich the cake halves together using the cream and redcurrants. Serve dusted with sifted icing sugar.

summer fruit & vanilla cake

Cuts into **16**
Preparation time **20 minutes**
Cooking time **40–45 minutes**

250 g (8 oz) **slightly salted butter**, softened
225 g (7½ oz) **caster sugar**, plus extra for sprinkling
3 **eggs**
2 teaspoons **vanilla bean paste** or **extract**
225 g (7½ oz) **self-raising flour**
150 g (5 oz) **ground almonds**
3 tablespoons **milk**
400 g (13 oz) **mixed fresh summer fruits**, such as **strawberries, raspberries** and **redcurrants**, halved or quartered if large

Beat together the butter, sugar, eggs, vanilla and flour in a bowl until pale and creamy. Stir in the ground almonds, milk and half the fruits.

Spoon the mixture into a greased and lined 28 x 24 cm (11 x 9¼ inch) shallow baking tin or roasting tin (see page 15) and level the surface. Scatter with the remaining fruits.

Bake in a preheated oven, 180°C (350°F), Gas Mark 4, for 40–45 minutes or until just firm to the touch and a skewer inserted into the centre comes out clean. Leave to cool in the tin, then transfer to a board and peel off the lining paper. Sprinkle with caster sugar and cut into squares.

For gooseberry & elderflower cake, top, tail and halve 350 g (11½ oz) fresh gooseberries and toss with 2 tablespoons caster sugar. Make the cake as above, replacing the summer fruits with the gooseberries and the milk with 3 tablespoons elderflower cordial. For the syrup, put 100 g (3½ oz) caster sugar and 4 tablespoons water in a small saucepan and heat gently until the sugar dissolves. Bring to the boil and boil for about 3–5 minutes until the syrup has thickened but is not beginning to colour. Remove from the heat, add 2 teaspoons lemon juice and 7 tablespoons elderflower cordial and stir well. Drizzle over the cooled cake and cut into squares.

squidgy apple cake

Cuts into **16**
Preparation time **20 minutes**
Cooking time **40–45 minutes**

250 g (8 oz) **slightly salted butter**, softened
250 g (8 oz) **golden caster sugar**, plus extra for sprinkling
2 teaspoons **ground mixed spice**
4 **eggs**
300 g (10 oz) **self-raising flour**
1 teaspoon **baking powder**
4 **tart dessert apples**

Beat together the butter, sugar, mixed spice, eggs, half of the flour and the baking powder in a bowl until pale and creamy. Peel 3 of the apples and coarsely grate into the bowl, stirring after each one is grated. Stir in the remaining flour.

Spoon the mixture into a greased and lined 32 x 22 cm (12½ x 8½ inch) shallow baking tin (see page 15) and level the surface. Peel and grate the remaining apple over the surface.

Bake in a preheated oven, 180°C (350°F), Gas Mark 4, for 40–45 minutes until golden, just firm to the touch and a skewer inserted into the centre comes out clean. Sprinkle with caster sugar and leave to cool in the tin. Peel off the lining paper and cut into squares, then serve, warm or cold, with Spiced Blackberry Sauce, if liked (see below).

For spiced blackberry sauce, to serve as an accompaniment, put 250 g (8 oz) fresh blackberries, 100 g (3½ oz) blackberry jam and 1 tablespoon lemon juice in a saucepan and heat gently for about 5 minutes until the blackberries have softened. Strain the sauce through a sieve, pressing the pulp with the back of a spoon to extract as much juice as possible. Serve warm or cold with the apple cake and extra blackberries.

plum & marzipan slice

Cuts into **8**
Preparation time **15 minutes**
Cooking time **25 minutes**

500 g (1 lb) **ready-made puff pastry**
250 g (8 oz) **white** or **golden marzipan**
800 g (1 lb 10 oz) **plums**, halved and stoned
beaten **egg**, to glaze

For the glaze
3 tablespoons **smooth apricot jam**
1 teaspoon **rosewater**
2 teaspoons **water**

Roll out the pastry on a lightly floured surface to a 35 x 20 cm (14 x 8 inch) rectangle. Place on a greased baking sheet. Using a sharp knife, score a 1.5 cm (¾ inch) border around the pastry edge. Roll out the marzipan on a surface lightly dusted with icing sugar to a 30 x 15 cm (12 x 6 inch) rectangle, then place inside the border. Arrange the plums over the marzipan. Brush the pastry border with beaten egg.

Bake in a preheated oven, 200°C (400°F), Gas Mark 6, for about 25 minutes until the pastry is risen and golden and the plums are tender.

Meanwhile, heat the glaze ingredients in a small saucepan, then brush over the plums. Serve warm or cold.

For strawberry custard slice, beat together 4 egg yolks, 50 g (2 oz) caster sugar, 1 teaspoon vanilla extract and 15 g (½ oz) plain flour in a heatproof bowl to make a paste. Bring 150 ml (¼ pint) milk and 150 ml (¼ pint) double cream to the boil in a saucepan. Pour over the yolk mixture, whisking well. Return to the saucepan and cook gently, stirring, for about 5 minutes until thickened and smooth. Leave to cool. Roll out the pastry to 30 x 18 cm (12 x 7 inches) and score as above, then bake for 20 minutes or until risen and deep golden. Leave to cool, then remove the pastry from inside the border to form a case. Spread the custard over the base and scatter with 400 g (13 oz) halved fresh strawberries. Heat 4 tablespoons strawberry jam and 1 tablespoon water in a saucepan. Strain through a sieve and drizzle over the strawberries.

rich chocolate brownies

Cuts into **15**
Preparation time **20 minutes**
Cooking time **35 minutes**

400 g (13 oz) **plain dark chocolate**
175 g (6 oz) **slightly salted butter**
3 **eggs**
225 g (7½ oz) **light muscovado sugar**
100 g (3½ oz) **self-raising flour**

Chop 150 g (5 oz) of the chocolate into 5 mm (¼ inch) pieces. Break the remaining chocolate into pieces and put in a heatproof bowl with the butter. Melt over a saucepan of gently simmering water (don't let the base of the bowl touch the water).

Beat the eggs and sugar in a separate bowl until light and foamy. Stir in the melted chocolate mixture. Tip in the flour and chopped chocolate and mix together until just combined.

Spoon the mixture into a greased and lined 28 x 18 cm (11 x 7 inch) shallow baking tin or roasting tin (see page 15) and level the surface. Bake in a preheated oven, 190°C (375°F), Gas Mark 5, for about 30 minutes or until a crust has formed but the mixture feels quite soft underneath. Leave to cool in the tin, then transfer to a board and cut into small squares. Peel off the lining paper.

For warm chocolate prune brownies, quarter 200 g (7 oz) stoned prunes and put in a bowl with 3 tablespoons brandy or white or dark rum. Leave to stand for several hours until the spirit has been absorbed. Make the brownie mixture as above, omitting the chopped chocolate and adding ½ teaspoon ground allspice. Stir in the steeped prunes and bake as above. Serve warm, cut into squares and topped with vanilla ice cream.

white chocolate & nut blondies

Cuts into **15**
Preparation time **20 minutes**
Cooking time **40 minutes**

- 400 g (13 oz) **white chocolate**, chopped
- 75 g (3 oz) **slightly salted butter**
- 3 **eggs**
- 175 g (6 oz) **light muscovado sugar**
- 150 g (5 oz) **self-raising flour**
- 150 g (5 oz) **unblanched hazelnuts** or **Brazil nuts**, chopped

Melt 100 g (3½ oz) of the chocolate and the butter in a heatproof bowl set over a saucepan of gently simmering water (don't let the base of the bowl touch the water).

Beat the eggs and sugar in a separate bowl until light and foamy. Stir in the melted chocolate mixture. Tip in the flour, remaining chopped chocolate and the nuts and mix together until just combined.

Spoon the mixture into a greased and lined 28 x 18 cm (11 x 7 inch) shallow baking tin or roasting tin (see page 15) and level the surface. Bake in a preheated oven, 190°C (375°F), Gas Mark 5, for about 35 minutes or until deep golden and just firm to the touch. Leave to cool in the tin, then transfer to a board and cut into small squares. Peel off the lining paper.

For frosted espresso blondies, dissolve 4 teaspoons instant espresso coffee powder or granules in 2 tablespoons boiling water. Make the brownies as above, omitting the 300 g (10 oz) chopped white chocolate, adding the coffee with the sugar and eggs and replacing the hazelnuts or Brazil nuts with 200 g (7 oz) chopped blanched almonds. For the frosting, heat 150 ml (¼ pint) double cream in a small saucepan until just boiling. Put 100 g (3½ oz) chopped white chocolate in a heatproof bowl and pour over the hot cream. Leave until the chocolate has melted, stirring frequently. Chill for 1 hour, then lightly whisk the mixture until it holds its shape. Spread over the cooled brownies and sprinkle with finely grated plain dark chocolate or drinking chocolate. Cut into small squares.

black forest brownies

Cuts into **12**
Preparation time **25 minutes**
Cooking time **25–30 minutes**

150 g (5 oz) **plain dark chocolate**, chopped
125 g (4 oz) **slightly salted butter**
2 **eggs**
175 g (6 oz) **dark muscovado sugar**
1 teaspoon **vanilla extract**
50 g (2 oz) **self-raising flour**
200 g (7 oz) **black** or **red cherries**, pitted and halved, plus extra to serve

To serve
150 ml (1/4 pint) **double cream**
chocolate shavings

Melt 50 g (2 oz) of the chocolate and the butter in a heatproof bowl set over a saucepan of gently simmering water (don't let the base of the bowl touch the water).

Beat the eggs, sugar and vanilla in a separate bowl until light and foamy. Stir in the melted chocolate mixture. Tip in the flour, cherries and remaining chocolate and mix together until just combined.

Spoon the mixture into a greased and lined 18 cm (7 inch) square cake tin or shallow baking tin (see page 15) and level the surface. Bake in a preheated oven, 180°C (350°F), Gas Mark 4, for 20–25 minutes or until just firm to the touch. Leave to cool in the tin, then transfer to a board and peel off the lining paper.

Whip the cream in a bowl until peaking, then spread over the cake. Sprinkle with chocolate shavings and cut into small squares. Serve with extra cherries and Rich Chocolate Sauce, if liked (see below).

For rich chocolate sauce, to serve as an accompaniment, heat 125 g (4 oz) caster sugar and 75 ml (3 fl oz) water in a small saucepan until the sugar dissolves. Bring to the boil and boil for 3 minutes. Remove from the heat and cool for 5 minutes. Add 150 g (5 oz) chopped plain dark chocolate and 25 g (1 oz) diced unsalted butter and leave to stand, stirring frequently, until melted and smooth. If pieces of chocolate remain, reheat the sauce very gently.

rum & raisin chocolate brownies

Cuts into **20**
Preparation time **30 minutes**, plus soaking
Cooking time **30–35 minutes**

- 3 tablespoons **white** or **dark rum**
- 100 g (3½ oz) **raisins**
- 250 g (8 oz) **plain dark chocolate**, broken into pieces
- 250 g (8 oz) **butter**
- 4 **eggs**
- 200 g (7 oz) **caster sugar**
- 75 g (3 oz) **self-raising flour**
- 1 teaspoon **baking powder**
- 100 g (3½ oz) **white** or **milk chocolate**, broken into pieces

Warm the rum gently in a small saucepan. Add the raisins and leave to soak for 2 hours or overnight. Heat the dark chocolate and butter gently in a saucepan until both have just melted, taking care not to scorch the chocolate.

Whisk together the eggs and sugar in a bowl using a hand-held electric whisk until the mixture is very thick and the whisk leaves a trail when lifted above it. Stir in the melted chocolate mixture. Sift in the flour and baking powder, then fold in.

Pour the mixture into a greased and lined 28 x 18 cm (11 x 7 inch) shallow baking tin or roasting tin (see page 15) and spread into the corners. Spoon the rum-soaked raisins over the top. Bake in a preheated oven, 180°C (350°F), Gas Mark 4, for 25–30 minutes until well risen; the top should be crusty and cracked and the centre still slightly soft. Leave to cool in the tin, then transfer to a board.

Melt the white or milk chocolate in a heatproof bowl set over a saucepan of gently simmering water (don't let the base of the bowl touch the water), then drizzle over the top of the brownies. Leave to harden, then cut into squares. Peel off the lining paper.

For triple chocolate brownies, make the brownie mixture as above, omitting the rum-soaked raisins. Pour into the tin, sprinkle with 100 g (3½ oz) finely chopped milk chocolate and 100 g (3½ oz) finely chopped white chocolate and bake as above. Omit the chocolate topping.

small cakes

raspberry ripple meringues

Makes about **12**
Preparation time **15 minutes**
Cooking time **1¼ hours**

40 g (1½ oz) **fresh raspberries**, plus extra to serve (optional)
2 tablespoons **raspberry jam**
4 **egg whites**
200 g (7 oz) **caster sugar**

Put the raspberries in a bowl and mash with a fork until broken up and turning juicy. Add the jam and mash together to make a purée. Tip into a sieve resting over a small bowl and press the purée with the back of a spoon to extract as much juice as possible.

Whisk the egg whites in a large clean bowl with a hand-held electric whisk until peaking. Whisk in a tablespoonful of the sugar and continue to whisk for about 15 seconds. Gradually add the remaining sugar, a spoonful at a time, until thick and glossy.

Drizzle over the raspberry purée and lightly stir in using a spatula or large metal spoon, scooping up the meringue from the base of the bowl so that the mixture is streaked with the purée. Take care not to over-mix.

Drop large spoonfuls of the mixture, each about the size of a small orange, on to a large baking sheet lined with baking parchment, then swirl with the back of a teaspoon. Bake in a preheated oven, 120°C (250°F), Gas Mark ½, for about 1¼ hours or until the meringues are crisp and come away easily from the paper. Leave to cool on the paper. Serve with extra raspberries, if liked.

For gingerbread meringues, put 5 tablespoons black treacle in a small bowl and stir in 2 teaspoons ground ginger, 1 teaspoon ground mixed spice and 1 teaspoon boiling water and mix well. Make the meringue mixture as above, replacing 50 g (2 oz) of the caster sugar with 50 g (2 oz) dark muscovado sugar, then ripple with the treacle syrup instead of the raspberry purée. Bake as above.

brown sugar meringues

Makes about **15**
Preparation time **25 minutes**
Cooking time **1 hour**

100 g (3½ oz) **light muscovado sugar**
75 g (3 oz) **caster sugar**
3 **egg whites**
200 g (7 oz) **clotted cream**

Mix together the sugars in a bowl. Whisk the egg whites in a large clean bowl with a hand-held electric whisk until peaking. Whisk in a tablespoonful of the sugar mixture and continue to whisk for about 15 seconds. Gradually add the remaining sugar, a spoonful at a time and whisking well between each addition, until thick and glossy.

Spoon about 30 dessertspoonfuls of the mixture into roughly swirled mounds on 2 baking sheets lined with baking parchment. Alternatively, spoon into a piping bag fitted with a nozzle and pipe swirls on to the baking sheets.

Bake in a preheated oven, 120°C (250°F), Gas Mark ½, for about 1 hour until the meringues are crisp and come away easily from the paper. Leave on the paper to cool, then use the clotted cream to sandwich the meringues together in pairs.

For chestnut meringue nests, make the meringue mixture as above and drop large spoonfuls, about the size of a small apple, on to the baking parchment. Flatten into a dome shape with a palette knife and push a deep cavity into the centre of each with the back of a teaspoon. Bake as above. Whip 200 ml (7 fl oz) extra- thick double cream in a bowl until peaking. Spoon on to the cooled meringues. Beat a squeeze of lemon juice into 150 g (5 oz) sweetened chestnut purée and spoon on to the meringues, then scatter with plain dark chocolate curls.

simple iced buns

Makes **10**
Preparation time **25 minutes**, plus proving
Cooking time **12–15 minutes**

500 g (1 lb) **strong white bread flour**
50 g (2 oz) **caster sugar**
1 tablespoon **fast-action dried yeast**
25 g (1 oz) **slightly salted butter**, melted
300 ml (½ pint) **hand-hot milk**, plus extra if required
2 teaspoons **vanilla extract**

For the icing
300 g (10 oz) **fondant icing sugar**
pink food colouring

Mix together the flour, sugar and yeast in a bowl. Add the butter, milk and vanilla and mix to a fairly soft dough, adding a dash more milk or hot water if the dough feels dry. Knead the dough for 10 minutes on a floured surface until smooth and elastic. Put in a lightly oiled bowl, cover with clingfilm and leave to rise in a warm place for about 1 hour or until doubled in size.

Punch the dough to deflate it, then divide into 10 even-sized pieces on a floured surface and shape each into a sausage shape. Place, well spaced apart, on a large greased baking sheet. Cover loosely with greased clingfilm and leave to rise for 30 minutes.

Bake in a preheated oven, 200°C (400°F), Gas Mark 6, for 12–15 minutes until risen and pale golden (placing a roasting tin filled with 1.5 cm (¾ inch) hot water on the lower shelf to prevent a firm crust forming). Transfer to a wire rack to cool.

Make the icing. Sift the icing sugar into a bowl and gradually beat in a little water, a teaspoonful at a time, to make a smooth, spreadable icing. Spread half over 5 of the buns. Add a dash of pink food colouring to the remaining icing and spread over the rest of the buns. Best eaten freshly baked.

For sticky currant buns, make the dough as above, adding ½ teaspoon ground cinnamon and 175 g (6 oz) mixed dried fruit. Leave to prove as above. Shape into 10 balls and flatten slightly on the baking sheet. Brush with a little milk and bake as above. Heat 2 tablespoons golden syrup in a saucepan and brush over the cooled buns.

mini custard tarts

Makes **12**
Preparation time **30 minutes**
Cooking time **35–40 minutes**

500 g (1 lb) **ready-made puff pastry**
1 tablespoon **vanilla sugar**
3 **eggs**
2 **egg yolks**
75 g (3 oz) **caster sugar**
1 teaspoon **vanilla bean paste** or **extract**
300 ml (½ pint) **single cream**
sifted **icing sugar**, for dusting

Roll out the pastry on a floured surface to 5 mm (¼ inch) thick. Cut in half and sprinkle one half with the vanilla sugar. Lay the second piece on top and thinly roll out the pastry. Cut out 12 rounds using a 9 cm (3¾ inch) plain biscuit cutter. Re-roll the trimmings to make more.

Press the rounds into the holes of a 12-hole nonstick muffin tray, pressing firmly into the sections. Line the pastry cases with squares of foil. (To do this, wrap each foil square tightly around half a lemon, then remove. Press the foil domes firmly into the pastry cases.)

Bake in a preheated oven, 200°C (400°F), Gas Mark 6, for 15 minutes. Remove the foil and bake the cases for a further 5 minutes until crisp. Reduce the oven temperature to 160°C (325°F), Gas Mark 3.

Meanwhile, beat together the eggs, egg yolks, caster sugar and vanilla in a heatproof bowl. Bring the cream to the boil in a saucepan and pour over the egg mixture, whisking well. Strain into a jug and pour into the cases. Bake in the oven for 15–20 minutes or until just set and still slightly wobbly in the centre. Leave to cool in the tin. Serve dusted with sifted icing sugar.

For lemon & treacle tarts, make and bake the pastry cases as above, omitting the vanilla sugar. Heat 400 g (13 oz) golden syrup in a saucepan until slightly thinned. Remove from the heat and beat in 75 g (3 oz) fresh white breadcrumbs, the finely grated rind of 2 lemons and 3 tablespoons lemon juice. Cool slightly, then beat in 1 egg and 1 egg yolk. Divide between the cases and return to the oven for 15 minutes until lightly set.

spiced eccles cakes

Makes **10**
Preparation time **20 minutes**
Cooking time **15 minutes**

175 g (6 oz) **currants**
25 g (1 oz) **candied peel**, finely chopped
½ teaspoon **ground mixed spice**
50 g (2 oz) **light muscovado sugar**
500 g (1 lb) **ready-made puff pastry**
beaten **egg**, to glaze
caster sugar, for sprinkling

Mix together the currants, candied peel, mixed spice and muscovado sugar in a bowl.

Roll out the pastry thinly on a lightly floured surface and cut out 10 rounds using a 12–13 cm (5–5½ inch) plain biscuit cutter or by cutting around a small bowl, re-rolling the trimmings to make more.

Brush the edges of the rounds with beaten egg and spoon the currant mixture into the centres. Bring the edges of the pastry up over the filling and pinch firmly together. Turn the cakes over and flatten under the palms of your hands. Place slightly apart on a large greased baking sheet and make several deep cuts over the top of each, through to the filling. Brush with beaten egg.

Bake in a preheated oven, 220°C (425°F), Gas Mark 7, for about 15 minutes until deep golden and puffed. Sprinkle with caster sugar, then transfer to a wire rack to cool.

For mincemeat & almond puffs, mix together 200 g (7 oz) mincemeat and 2 tablespoons almond liqueur. Leave to stand for at least 2 hours, then stir in 25 g (1 oz) crumbled flaked almonds. Make the pastries as above, using the mincemeat as a filling. Serve warm or cold with pouring cream or ice cream.

cheat's lemon dainties

Cuts into **9**
Preparation time **25 minutes**, plus chilling

8 **trifle sponges**, sliced in half horizontally to give shallower pieces
100 g (3½ oz) **butter**, softened
100 g (3½ oz) **caster sugar**
grated rind of 2 **lemons**
2 **eggs**, separated
150 ml (¼ pint) **double cream**
juice of 1 **lemon**

To serve
125 g (4 oz) **fresh raspberries**
100 g (3½ oz) **fresh blueberries**
mint leaves
4 tablespoons **icing sugar**, sifted

Arrange half of the trifle sponges in a single layer in the base of a 20 cm (8 inch) square shallow cake tin lined with clingfilm.

Beat together the butter, sugar and lemon rind until pale and creamy. Gradually beat in the egg yolks.

Whisk the egg whites in a large clean bowl with a hand-held electric whisk until stiff, then whip the cream in a separate bowl. Fold the whipped cream and the egg whites into the creamed mixture. Gradually fold in the juice of ½ lemon.

Drizzle a little of the remaining lemon juice over the trifle sponges. Spoon the cream mixture on top and gently spread the surface level. Cover with a second layer of sponge slices, press them gently into the cream mixture and drizzle with the remaining lemon juice. Cover with an extra piece of clingfilm and chill for 4 hours or overnight.

Remove the top layer of clingfilm, invert the cake on to a board and peel off the remaining clingfilm. Cut into squares, decorate with berries and mint leaves and serve dusted with the sifted icing sugar.

For tiramisu squares, mix 4 tablespoons strong black coffee with 2 tablespoons sherry. Spoon half over the trifle sponges in the tin. Beat together 250 g (8 oz) mascarpone cheese, 50 g (2 oz) caster sugar and 150 ml (¼ pint) double cream in a bowl. Spoon half into the tin and sprinkle with 50 g (2 oz) chopped plain dark chocolate, then repeat the layering with the remaining ingredients and a further 50 g (2 oz) chocolate sprinkled over the top. Cover and chill before serving.

vanilla fudge nuggets

Makes **16**
Preparation time **15 minutes**, plus chilling
Cooking time **15–20 minutes**

- 75 g (3 oz) **unsalted butter**, softened
- 75 g (3 oz) **golden caster sugar**
- 1 **egg yolk**
- 1 tablespoon **egg white**
- 150 g (5 oz) **self-raising flour,** sifted
- 8 pieces of **soft vanilla fudge**, halved
- sifted **icing sugar**, for dusting

Beat together the butter and caster sugar in a bowl until pale and fluffy. Beat in the egg yolk and white, then add the flour and mix to a firm dough. Knead into a ball, wrap in clingfilm and chill for at least 30 minutes.

Divide the dough in half, then press half the dough into 16 mini silicone muffin cases arranged on a baking sheet. Push a piece of fudge down into the centre of each case. Divide the remaining dough into 16 pieces. Roll each piece into a ball using lightly floured hands and flatten into a round roughly 5 cm (2 inches) in diameter. Push a round of dough into each case, covering the fudge, and press it down firmly around the edge.

Bake in a preheated oven, 190°C (375°F), Gas Mark 5, for 15–20 minutes or until slightly risen. Leave to cool in the cases for 5 minutes, then transfer to a wire rack to cool completely. Serve lightly dusted with sifted icing sugar.

For double-choc nuggets, make the nuggets as above, replacing 25 g (1 oz) of the flour with 25 g (1 oz) cocoa powder and the pieces of fudge with 16 squares of plain dark or milk chocolate. Serve lightly dusted with sifted cocoa powder.

scones with jam & cream

Makes **10**
Preparation time **15 minutes**
Cooking time **12 minutes**

225 g (7½ oz) **self-raising flour**
1 teaspoon **baking powder**
40 g (1½ oz) **slightly salted butter**, chilled and diced
2 tablespoons **caster sugar**
125 ml (4 fl oz) **milk**, plus extra to glaze

To serve
strawberry jam
clotted cream

Sift the flour and baking powder into a bowl or food processor. Add the butter and rub in with the fingertips or process until the mixture resembles fine breadcrumbs. Add the sugar and milk, reserving 2 tablespoons of milk, and mix or blend briefly to a soft, slightly sticky dough. Add the reserved milk if the dough feels dry.

Knead the dough lightly on a lightly floured surface until smooth, then roll out to 1.5 cm (¾ inch) thick. Cut out 10 rounds using a 5 cm (2 inch) plain biscuit cutter, re-rolling the trimmings to make more. Place slightly apart on a greased baking sheet and brush with milk.

Bake in a preheated oven, 220°C (425°F), Gas Mark 7, for 12 minutes until well risen and golden. Transfer to a wire rack to cool.

Split the scones and serve topped with jam and cream.

For maple & raisin scones, make the dough as above, omitting the sugar and replacing 75 ml (3 fl oz) of the milk with 75 ml (3 fl oz) maple syrup. Stir in 65 g (2½ oz) raisins. Mix together 2 teaspoons maple syrup and 2 teaspoons milk in a small bowl. Cut out the scones as above, then brush with the maple syrup mixture. Bake as above and serve buttered.

lavender tea scones

Makes **24**
Preparation time **20 minutes**
Cooking time **8–10 minutes**

225 g (7½ oz) **self-raising flour**
1 teaspoon **baking powder**
4 **lavender flower stems**
40 g (1½ oz) **unsalted butter**, chilled and diced
150 ml (¼ pint) **buttermilk**
milk or **beaten egg**, to glaze
caster sugar, for sprinkling

For the filling
150 ml (¼ pint) **double cream**
4 tablespoons **strawberry jam**

Sift the flour and baking powder into a bowl or food processor. Pull the lavender flowers from the stems and add with the butter. Rub in the butter with the fingertips or process until the mixture resembles breadcrumbs. Add the buttermilk and mix or blend briefly to a soft dough.

Knead the dough on a lightly floured surface until smooth, then roll out to 1.5 cm (¾ inch) thick. Cut out 24 rounds using a 3 cm (1¼ inch) plain biscuit cutter, re-rolling the trimmings to make more. Place slightly apart on a greased baking sheet, brush with milk or beaten egg and sprinkle with caster sugar.

Bake in a preheated oven, 220°C (425°F), Gas Mark 7, for 8–10 minutes until risen and pale golden. Transfer to a wire rack to cool.

Whip the cream in a bowl until just holding its shape. Split the scones and sandwich together with the jam and whipped cream.

For cranberry & orange scones, chop 50 g (2 oz) dried cranberries and steep in 2 tablespoons orange juice until the juice is absorbed. Make the scones as above, adding ¼ teaspoon ground mixed spice with the flour, and the cranberries and the finely grated rind of 1 small orange with the buttermilk. Serve warm, split and buttered.

sweet carrot & rosemary scones

Makes **22–24**
Preparation time **15 minutes**
Cooking time **8–10 minutes**

225 g (7½ oz) **stoneground spelt flour**
2 teaspoons **baking powder**
½ teaspoon **cream of tartar**
2 teaspoons finely chopped **rosemary**
2 tablespoons **caster sugar**
50 g (2 oz) **slightly salted butter**, chilled and diced
125 g (4 oz) **small carrots,** finely grated
100 ml (3½ fl oz) **milk**, plus extra to glaze

To serve
mascarpone cheese
fruit jelly, such as **crab apple, apple** or **orange**

Sift the flour, baking powder and cream of tartar into a bowl or food processor, tipping in the grains left in the sieve. Stir in the rosemary and sugar. Add the butter and rub in with the fingertips or process until the mixture resembles breadcrumbs. Stir in the grated carrots and milk and mix or blend briefly to a soft dough, adding a dash more milk if the dough feels dry.

Knead the dough on a lightly floured surface until smooth, then roll out to 1.5 cm (¾ inch) thick. Cut out 22–24 rounds using a 3 cm (1¼ inch) plain biscuit cutter, re-rolling the trimmings to make more. Place slightly apart on a greased baking sheet and brush with milk.

Bake in a preheated oven, 220°C (425°F), Gas Mark 7, for 8–10 minutes until risen and pale golden. Transfer to a wire rack to cool.

Split the scones and serve spread with mascarpone and fruit jelly.

For wholemeal apple & sultana scones, mix 125 g (4 oz) plain wholemeal flour, 100 g (3½ oz) self-raising flour, 1 teaspoon ground mixed spice and 2 teaspoons baking powder in a bowl or food processor. Add 40 g (1½ oz) slightly salted butter, chilled and diced, and rub in with the fingertips or process until the mixture resembles breadcrumbs. Stir or blend in 50 g (2 oz) chopped sultanas and 1 peeled, cored and grated dessert apple. Add 125 ml (4 fl oz) milk and mix or blend to a soft dough, adding a little more milk if the dough feels dry. Roll out, shape and bake as above.

fruited friands

Makes **12**
Preparation time **20 minutes**, plus cooling
Cooking time **25 minutes**

175 g (6 oz) **unsalted butter**
75 g (3 oz) **dried strawberries, sour cherries** or **cranberries** roughly chopped
2 tablespoons **orange juice**
6 **egg whites**
225 g (7½ oz) **caster sugar**, plus extra for sprinkling
75 g (3 oz) **plain flour**
125 g (4 oz) **ground almonds**

Melt the butter and leave to cool (see pages 15–16). Put the strawberries, cherries or cranberries and orange juice in a saucepan and heat until the mixture is hot, then turn into a bowl and leave to cool.

Whisk the egg whites in a large clean bowl with a hand-held electric whisk until frothy and increased in volume but not peaking. Add the sugar, flour and ground almonds and stir in until almost combined. Drizzle the melted butter over the mixture, then stir together gently until just combined.

Divide the mixture evenly between the holes of a greased 12-hole muffin tray, then scatter the strawberries, cherries or cranberries on top. Bake in a preheated oven, 200°C (400°F), Gas Mark 6, for about 20 minutes until pale golden and just firm to the touch. Leave in the tin for 5 minutes, then transfer to a wire rack to cool. Serve sprinkled with caster sugar.

For hazelnut friands, put 125 g (4 oz) blanched hazelnuts in a food processor or blender and whizz until the consistency of ground almonds. Finely chop a further 25 g (1 oz) hazelnuts. Make the friands as above, adding ½ teaspoon ground cinnamon when melting the butter, omitting the strawberries and orange juice and replacing the ground almonds with the ground hazelnuts. Spoon the mixture into the tray and scatter with the chopped hazelnuts. Bake as above.

rock buns

Makes **18–20**
Preparation time **15 minutes**
Cooking time **15–20 minutes**

125 g (4 oz) **slightly salted butter**, softened
100 g (3½ oz) **demerara sugar**, plus extra for sprinkling
225 g (7½ oz) **self-raising flour**
2 teaspoons **ground mixed spice**
1 **egg**
150 ml (¼ pint) **buttermilk**
175 g (6 oz) **raisins**

Beat together the butter and sugar in a bowl until pale and fluffy. Add the remaining ingredients and mix until evenly combined.

Using 2 forks, place small heaps of the mixture, spaced slightly apart, on 2 greased baking sheets. Sprinkle with extra demerara sugar.

Bake in a preheated oven, 190°C (375°F), Gas Mark 5, for 15–20 minutes or until deep golden. Transfer to a wire rack to cool. Serve on the same day.

For coconut & cherry buns, make the buns as above, replacing 50 g (2 oz) of the flour with 25 g (1 oz) desiccated coconut, omitting the mixed spice and adding 150 g (5 oz) roughly chopped natural glacé cherries instead of the raisins. Omit the extra sugar for sprinkling. Beat a dash of water into 75 g (3 oz) sifted icing sugar to make a thick, spoonable icing. Drizzle over the cooled buns to serve.

muffins & cupcakes

very chocolatey muffins

Makes **12**
Preparation time **20 minutes**
Cooking time **25 minutes**

175 g (6 oz) **plain dark chocolate**, broken into pieces
50 g (2 oz) **slightly salted butter**
275 g (9 oz) **self-raising flour**
1 tablespoon **baking powder**
50 g (2 oz) **cocoa powder**
125 g (4 oz) **light muscovado sugar**
150 g (5 oz) **milk chocolate**, chopped
1 **egg**, beaten
2 teaspoons **vanilla extract**
275 ml (9 fl oz) **milk**

Melt the plain dark chocolate and butter in a heatproof bowl set over a saucepan of gently simmering water (don't let the base of the bowl touch the water).

Mix together the flour, baking powder, cocoa powder, sugar and milk chocolate in a large bowl. Beat together the egg, vanilla and milk in a jug. Pour a little into the melted chocolate and stir well until smooth. Stir in the remaining milk mixture, then pour into the dry ingredients. Stir together using a large metal spoon until just combined.

Divide the mixture evenly between paper muffin cases arranged in a 12-hole muffin tray. Bake in a preheated oven, 190°C (375°F), Gas Mark 5, for about 20 minutes until well risen and just firm to the touch. Transfer to a wire rack to cool, then serve warm or cold.

For warm fudge muffins, mix together 400 g (13 oz) self-raising flour, 1 tablespoon baking powder, 100 g (3½ oz) golden caster sugar and 200 g (7 oz) diced fudge sweets in a bowl. Beat together 2 eggs, 50 g (2 oz) melted butter, 200 ml (7 fl oz) milk and 2 teaspoons vanilla extract in a jug. Add to the dry ingredients and continue as above.

chilli chocolate chip muffins

Makes **8**
Preparation time **20 minutes**
Cooking time **20 minutes**

200 g (7 oz) **self-raising flour**
50 g (2 oz) **cocoa powder**
1 teaspoon **baking powder**
150 g (5 oz) **soft light brown sugar**
1 **egg**, lightly beaten
250 ml (8 fl oz) **milk**
50 g (2 oz) **butter**, melted
125 g (4 oz) **chilli chocolate**, chopped, or **plain dark chocolate**, chopped, and a **pinch of chilli powder**
75 g (3 oz) **pecan nuts**, toasted and roughly ground
spray olive oil, for oiling

Cut a 15 cm (6 inch) square from baking parchment and use it as a template to cut 7 more. Fold them all into quarters. Open out flat and set aside.

Sift the flour, cocoa powder and baking powder into a bowl and stir in the sugar. Beat together the egg, milk and melted butter in a jug. Add to the dry ingredients and stir together using a large metal spoon until just combined. Fold in the chocolate or chocolate and chilli powder and pecan nuts.

Spray each square of baking parchment with spray oil and press each piece into the hole of a muffin tray. Spoon the chocolate mixture into the lined holes and bake in a preheated oven, 200°C (400°F), Gas Mark 6, for 20 minutes until risen and golden. Transfer to a wire rack to cool slightly, then serve warm.

For white chocolate & raspberry muffins, make the muffin mixture as above, replacing the cocoa powder with an extra 50 g (2 oz) self-raising flour. Omit the chilli chocolate or chocolate and chilli powder and pecans and fold in 125 g (4 oz) chopped white chocolate and 125 g (4 oz) small raspberries. Bake as above and serve warm.

banana & chocolate muffins

Makes **12**
Preparation time **15 minutes**
Cooking time **20–25 minutes**

150 g (5 oz) **self-raising wholemeal flour**
150 g (5 oz) **plain flour**
1 teaspoon **baking powder**
1 teaspoon **bicarbonate of soda**
½ teaspoon **salt**
125 g (4 oz) **golden caster sugar**
3 large **ripe bananas**, mashed
1 **egg**, beaten
75 ml (3 fl oz) **water**
75 ml (3 fl oz) **vegetable oil**
75 g (3 oz) **carob** or **plain dark chocolate**, roughly chopped

Sift the flours, baking powder, bicarbonate of soda and salt into a large bowl, tipping in the wheatgerm left in the sieve. Stir in the sugar. Mix together the bananas, egg, measurement water and oil in a jug. Add to the dry ingredients and stir together using a large metal spoon until just combined. Fold in the carob or chocolate.

Divide the mixture evenly between ramekins or paper muffin cases arranged in a 12-hole muffin tray. Bake in a preheated oven, 180°C (350°F), Gas Mark 4, for 20–25 minutes until they are well risen and spring back when pressed. Transfer to a wire rack to cool.

For fresh cherry & vanilla muffins, make the muffins as above, replacing the bananas with 2 teaspoons vanilla extract and the carob or chocolate with 250 g (8 oz) pitted cherries.

rhubarb & marzipan muffins

Makes **12**
Preparation time **20 minutes**, plus cooling
Cooking time **30 minutes**

400 g (13 oz) **young rhubarb**, trimmed and cut into 1 cm (½ inch) lengths
100 g (3½ oz) **caster sugar**, plus extra 3 tablespoons
375 g (12 oz) **self-raising flour**
2 teaspoons **baking powder**
150 g (5 oz) **golden marzipan**, diced
2 **eggs**, beaten
100 g (3½ oz) **slightly salted butter**, melted
150 ml (¼ pint) **milk**
sifted **icing sugar**, for sprinkling

Toss the rhubarb with the 3 tablespoons sugar. Tip on to a baking sheet lined with baking parchment. Bake in a preheated oven, 200°C (400°F), Gas Mark 6, for 10 minutes until softened. Leave to cool.

Put the remaining sugar in a bowl with the flour and baking powder. Stir in the marzipan and cooled rhubarb. Beat together the eggs, melted butter and milk in a jug. Add to the dry ingredients and stir together using a large metal spoon until just combined.

Divide the mixture evenly between paper muffin cases arranged in a 12-hole muffin tray. Bake for about 20 minutes until well risen and just firm to the touch. Transfer to a wire rack to cool, then serve warm or cold, sprinkled with sifted icing sugar.

For plum & cinnamon muffins, halve, stone and dice 400 g (13 oz) ripe plums. Make the muffin mixture as above, replacing 50 g (2 oz) of the flour with 50 g (2 oz) ground almonds and 1 teaspoon ground cinnamon, stirring in the diced plums instead of the rhubarb and adding ½ teaspoon almond extract with the milk. Spoon the mixture into the muffin cases and sprinkle with demerara sugar. Bake as above.

raspberry muffins

Makes **6**
Preparation time **15 minutes**
Cooking time **15–20 minutes**

200 g (7 oz) **plain flour**
75 g (3 oz) **caster sugar**
2 tablespoons **ground almonds**
2 teaspoons **baking powder**
grated rind of 1 **lemon**
150 ml (1/4 pint) **buttermilk**
1 egg, beaten
50 g (2 oz) **butter**, melted
150 g (5 oz) **fresh** or **frozen raspberries**

Mix together the flour, sugar, ground almonds, baking powder and lemon rind in a large bowl. Mix together the buttermilk, egg, melted butter and raspberries in a jug. Add to the dry ingredients and stir together using a large metal spoon until just combined and slightly lumpy.

Divide the mixture evenly between 6 paper muffin cases arranged in a 12-hole muffin tray and bake in a preheated oven, 180°C (350°F), Gas Mark 4, for 15–20 minutes until risen and golden.

For blackcurrant crunch muffins, make the muffin mixture as above, replacing the raspberries with 150 g (5 oz) fresh blackcurrants. Spoon the mixture into the muffin cases and sprinkle the tops with 1 tablespoon chopped blanched hazelnuts and 1 tablespoon demerara sugar. Bake as above.

best blueberry muffins

Makes **12**
Preparation time **15 minutes**
Cooking time **20 minutes**

275 g (9 oz) **self-raising flour**
2 teaspoons **baking powder**
100 g (3½ oz) **caster sugar**
250 g (8 oz) **fresh blueberries**
2 **eggs**, beaten
50 g (2 oz) **slightly salted butter**, melted
200 ml (7 fl oz) **milk**
2 teaspoons **vanilla bean paste** or **extract**
vanilla sugar, for sprinkling

Mix together the flour, baking powder and caster sugar in a bowl. Stir in the blueberries. Beat together the eggs, melted butter, milk and vanilla in a jug. Add to the dry ingredients and stir together using a large metal spoon until just combined.

Divide the mixture evenly between paper muffin cases arranged in a 12-hole muffin tray. Bake in a preheated oven, 200°C (400°F), Gas Mark 6, for about 20 minutes until well risen and just firm to the touch. Transfer to a wire rack and sprinkle with vanilla sugar. Serve warm or cold.

For cranberry & oat muffins, mix together 150 g (5 oz) self-raising flour, 100 g (3½ oz) plain wholemeal flour, 75 g (3 oz) porridge oats, 1 tablespoon baking powder, 1 teaspoon ground ginger and 100 g (3½ oz) light muscovado sugar in a bowl. Stir in 150 g (5 oz) dried cranberries. Beat together 2 eggs, 6 tablespoons mild olive or vegetable oil, 150 ml (¼ pint) milk and 4 pieces of stem ginger in syrup, finely chopped, in a jug. Add to the dry ingredients and continue as above.

flower cupcakes

Makes **12**
Preparation time **40 minutes**, plus cooling
Cooking time **20–25 minutes**

150 g (5 oz) **slightly salted butter**, softened
150 g (5 oz) **caster sugar**
2 **eggs**
1½ tablespoons **rosewater**
1 tablespoon **milk**
175 g (6 oz) **self-raising flour**

For the icing
150 g (5 oz) **white chocolate,** broken into pieces
25 g (1 oz) **slightly salted butter**

To decorate
50 g (2 oz) **pink ready-to-roll icing**
50 g (2 oz) **yellow ready-to-roll icing**
icing sugar, for dusting, if liked

Beat together all the cake ingredients in a bowl until smooth and creamy. Divide the mixture evenly between paper cupcake cases arranged in a 12-hole cupcake tray. Bake in a preheated oven, 180°C (350°F), Gas Mark 4, for 20–25 minutes until risen and just firm to the touch. Transfer to a wire rack to cool.

Make the icing. Melt the chocolate and butter in a heatproof bowl set over a saucepan of gently simmering water (don't let the base of the bowl touch the water). Leave to cool and thicken slightly, then spread over the tops of the cupcakes.

Take a ball of pink icing, about the size of a small cherry, and roll between the palms of your hands until it is about 9 cm (3½ inches) long. Press the icing flat with your fingers, particularly along the top edge, then roll up the icing to make a simple rose shape. Slice off the base and press gently on to a cake. Repeat with the remaining icing until all the cakes are topped with a flower. Serve dusted with icing sugar.

For button cupcakes, make the cupcakes as above, replacing the rosewater with 1 teaspoon vanilla extract. Thinly roll out 50 g (2 oz) each of red, green and blue ready-to-roll icing on a surface dusted with sifted icing sugar. Cut out rounds using a 1–1.5 cm (½–¾ inch) plain cutter. Place on a baking sheet lined with baking parchment and press 4 holes into the centre of each with a cocktail stick or metal skewer. Leave for at least 2 hours to set. Beat 300 g (10 oz) sifted fondant icing sugar with enough water to make a smooth, spreadable icing. Spread over the cooled cupcakes, then decorate with the icing buttons.

pecan & muscovado cupcakes

Makes **12**
Preparation time **30 minutes**
Cooking time **18–20 minutes**

200 g (7 oz) **pecan nuts**
3 **eggs**, separated, plus 1 **egg white**
150 g (5 oz) **light muscovado sugar**
50 g (2 oz) **fresh white breadcrumbs**
50 g (2 oz) **unsalted butter**, melted

For the buttercream
100 g (3½ oz) **unsalted butter**, softened
175 g (6 oz) **light muscovado sugar**
1 teaspoon **vanilla bean paste** or **extract**
1 teaspoon **boiling water**

Reserve 12 of the pecan halves. Put the remaining nuts in a food processor and whizz until the consistency of ground almonds. Add the egg yolks, 100 g (3½ oz) of the sugar, the breadcrumbs and melted butter and blend until smooth. Turn into a bowl.

Whisk the egg whites in a large clean bowl with a hand-held electric whisk until peaking. Gradually whisk in the remaining sugar, a spoonful at a time. Stir a third of the mixture into the pecan mixture using a large metal spoon. Add the remaining egg whites and stir gently until just combined.

Divide the mixture evenly between paper cupcake cases arranged in a 12-hole cupcake tray. Bake in a preheated oven, 180°C (350°F), Gas Mark 4, for 18–20 minutes until just firm to the touch. Leave to cool for 10 minutes, then transfer to a wire rack to cool completely.

Make the buttercream. Beat together the butter, sugar and vanilla until pale and creamy. Add the measurement water and beat again until paler in colour. Spread over the cupcakes and decorate each with a pecan half.

For peanut butter cupcakes, beat together 125 g (4 oz) softened slightly salted butter, 125 g (4 oz) caster sugar, 2 eggs, 125 g (4 oz) self-raising flour and 2 tablespoons milk in a bowl, then stir in 100 g (3½ oz) finely chopped salted peanuts. Bake as above. For the icing, beat together 75 g (3 oz) smooth peanut butter, 50 g (2 oz) softened unsalted butter and 100 g (3½ oz) sifted icing sugar until smooth. Beat in 1 teaspoon boiling water. Spread over the cooled cupcakes and scatter with extra chopped peanuts.

lemon & cardamom cupcakes

Makes **12**
Preparation time **25 minutes**
Cooking time **20–25 minutes**

1 tablespoon **cardamom pods**
finely grated rind of 2 **lemons**
150 g (5 oz) **caster sugar**
150 g (5 oz) **slightly salted butter**, softened
2 **eggs**
175 g (6 oz) **self-raising flour**
1 tablespoon **lemon juice**
chopped **lemon jellies**, to decorate

For the icing
175 g (6 oz) **icing sugar**, sifted
2 tablespoons **lemon juice**
yellow food colouring (optional)

Crush the cardamom pods using a pestle and mortar or a small bowl and the end of a rolling pin. Discard the husks and crush the seeds as finely as possible.

Reserve ¼ teaspoon of the crushed seeds for the decoration and put the remaining seeds in a food processor with the lemon rind and sugar. Process lightly until the sugar is almost powdered. Add the butter, eggs, flour and lemon juice. Blend until soft and creamy, scraping the mixture down from the side of the bowl.

Divide the mixture evenly between paper cupcake cases arranged in a 12-hole cupcake tray. Bake in a preheated oven, 180°C (350°F), Gas Mark 4, for 20–25 minutes until just firm to the touch. Transfer to a wire rack to cool.

Make the icing. Beat together the icing sugar and lemon juice in a bowl until combined. Add a dash of yellow food colouring, if using, and a few drops of water or extra lemon juice to make a smooth, spreadable icing. Spread over the cupcakes, then decorate with chopped lemon jellies and sprinkle with the reserved cardamom.

For orange & passion fruit cupcakes, make the cupcakes as above, omitting the cardamom and replacing the lemon rind and juice with the finely grated rind of 1 orange and 1 tablespoon orange juice. For the icing, scoop the pulp from 3 ripe passion fruit into a bowl. Press the pulp through a sieve, if liked, to extract the seeds. Add 175 g (6 oz) sifted icing sugar and mix well to make a smooth, spreadable icing. Spread over the cooled cupcakes.

amaretti cupcakes

Makes **12**
Preparation time **15 minutes**
Cooking time **20–25 minutes**

125 g (4 oz) **amaretti biscuits**
125 g (4 oz) **caster sugar**
175 g (6 oz) **unsalted butter**, softened
3 **eggs**
125 g (4 oz) **self-raising flour**
½ teaspoon **baking powder**
3 tablespoons **flaked almonds**
sifted **icing sugar**, for dusting

Put the amaretti biscuits in a plastic bag and crush with a rolling pin until almost powdered. Tip the biscuits into a bowl and add the sugar, butter, eggs, flour and baking powder. Beat together until smooth and creamy.

Divide the mixture evenly between paper cupcake cases arranged in a 12-hole cupcake tray and roughly level with the back of a teaspoon. Scatter with the flaked almonds.

Bake in a preheated oven, 180°C (350°F), Gas Mark 4, for 20–25 minutes until risen and just firm to the touch. Transfer to a wire rack to cool. Serve dusted with sifted icing sugar.

For spiced ratafia cupcakes, make the cupcakes as above, replacing the amaretti biscuits with 125 g (4 oz) ratafia biscuits and adding 1 teaspoon ground mixed spice with the flour. For brandy butter, beat together 100 g (3½ oz) softened unsalted butter and 125 g (4 oz) sifted icing sugar until smooth, then add 3 tablespoons brandy and beat until pale and creamy. Spread over the cooled cupcakes.

elderflower cupcakes

Makes **12**
Preparation time **15 minutes**
Cooking time **20–25 minutes**

150 g (5 oz) **slightly salted butter**, very soft
150 g (5 oz) **caster sugar**
2 **eggs**
2 tablespoons **elderflower cordial** (see below for homemade)
finely grated rind of 1 **lemon**
175 g (6 oz) **self-raising flour**
elderflower sprigs, to decorate (if available)

For the frosting
250 g (8 oz) **cream cheese**
50 g (2 oz) **unsalted butter**, softened
100–125 ml (3½–4 fl oz) **elderflower cordial**

Beat together all the cake ingredients in a bowl until smooth and creamy. Divide the mixture evenly between paper cupcake cases arranged in a 12-hole cupcake tray.

Bake in a preheated oven, 180°C (350°F), Gas Mark 4, for 20–25 minutes until risen and just firm to the touch. Transfer to a wire rack to cool.

Make the frosting. Beat the cream cheese in a bowl until softened and smooth. Add the butter and most of the elderflower cordial and beat until smooth and creamy. Add more cordial if the frosting will absorb it without losing its shape. Spread over the cupcakes and decorate with elderflower sprigs, if using.

For homemade elderflower cordial, put 20 elderflower heads, 3 sliced lemons and 25 g (1 oz) citric acid in a large heatproof bowl. Dissolve 1 kg (2 lb) granulated or caster sugar in 1 litre (1¾ pints) boiling water, stirring frequently until dissolved. Add to the bowl of elderflowers. Cover and leave to stand overnight. Strain through a muslin-lined sieve and pour into sterilized bottles. Store in a cool place and use within 6 months.

coconut & mango cupcakes

Makes **12**
Preparation time **25 minutes**, plus standing
Cooking time **25 minutes**

150 g (5 oz) **dried mango**, chopped
finely grated rind of 1 **orange**
6 tablespoons **orange juice**
50 g (2 oz) **creamed coconut**, grated
175 g (6 oz) **slightly salted butter**, softened
150 g (5 oz) **caster sugar**
2 **eggs**
175 g (6 oz) **self-raising flour**
toasted desiccated or **shredded coconut**, to decorate

For the frosting
50 ml (2 fl oz) **single cream**
40 g (1½ oz) **creamed coconut**
2 teaspoons **lemon juice**
250 g (8 oz) **icing sugar**, sifted

Put the mango, orange rind and juice in a small bowl and leave to stand for several hours until the juice has been absorbed.

Soften the creamed coconut briefly in the microwave if firm, or alternatively grate it. Put the creamed coconut, butter, sugar, eggs and flour in a bowl and beat until smooth and creamy. Add the steeped mango and any juice left in the bowl.

Divide the mixture evenly between paper cupcake cases arranged in a 12-hole cupcake tray. Bake in a preheated oven, 180°C (350°F) Gas Mark 4, for about 20 minutes until risen and just firm to the touch. Transfer to a wire rack to cool.

Make the frosting. Heat the cream and creamed coconut in a small saucepan until the coconut has melted. Pour into a bowl, add the lemon juice and icing sugar and whisk together until smooth. Spread over the cupcakes and decorate with toasted coconut.

For cranberry & coconut cupcakes, mix together 150 g (5 oz) roughly chopped fresh cranberries and 50 g (2 oz) icing sugar in a bowl. Leave to stand for 30 minutes, then make the cupcakes as above, replacing the mango with the cranberries. For the icing, beat together 100 g (3½ oz) sifted icing sugar and 1 tablespoon water until smooth. Add a dash more water if necessary to make a thick, spoonable icing. Scribble the icing over the cooled cupcakes.

chocolate & raspberry cupcakes

Makes **12**
Preparation time **25 minutes**, plus cooling
Cooking time **35 minutes**

50 g (2 oz) **plain dark chocolate**, chopped
100 ml (3½ fl oz) **water**
125 g (4 oz) **unsalted butter**, softened
200 g (7 oz) **light muscovado sugar**
2 **eggs**
175 g (6 oz) **plain flour**
25 g (1 oz) **cocoa powder**
1 teaspoon **bicarbonate of soda**
½ teaspoon **baking powder**
100 ml (3½ fl oz) **soured cream**
12 **fresh raspberries**, to decorate

For the ganache
200 ml (7 fl oz) **double cream**
2 tablespoons **icing sugar**
200 g (7 oz) **plain dark chocolate**, chopped
100 g (3½ oz) **fresh raspberries**, halved

Put the chocolate and measurement water in a small saucepan and heat gently until the chocolate has melted. Leave to cool.

Beat together the butter, sugar, eggs, flour, cocoa powder, bicarbonate of soda and baking powder in a bowl until smooth and creamy. Add the cooled chocolate and soured cream and stir until evenly combined.

Divide the mixture evenly between paper cupcake cases arranged in a 12-hole cupcake tray. Bake in a preheated oven, 180°C (350°F), Gas Mark 4, for about 25 minutes until risen and just firm to the touch. Transfer to a wire rack to cool.

Make the ganache. Heat the cream and icing sugar in a saucepan until bubbling around the edge. Pour over the chopped chocolate in a heatproof bowl and leave until the chocolate has melted, stirring frequently. Cover and chill until beginning to thicken. Stir in the raspberries and spoon over the cupcakes. Top each cake with a fresh raspberry.

For white chocolate ganache, to use instead of the raspberry ganache, heat 100 ml (3½ fl oz) double cream in a small saucepan until bubbling around the edge. Remove from the heat and stir in 200 g (7 oz) chopped white chocolate. Turn into a bowl and leave until the chocolate has melted. Stir in another 100 ml (3½ fl oz) double cream and chill for at least 2 hours. Beat with a balloon or hand-held electric whisk until thickened. Spread over the cupcakes and scatter with plain dark or white chocolate curls.

peanut caramel cupcakes

Makes **16**
Preparation time **20 minutes**
Cooking time **15–20 minutes**

65 g (2½ oz) **slightly salted butter**, softened
65 g (2½ oz) **light muscovado sugar**
65 g (2½ oz) **self-raising flour**
1 **egg**
50 g (2 oz) **salted peanuts**, finely chopped, plus extra to decorate

For the frosting
50 g (2 oz) **slightly salted butter**
100 g (3½ oz) **light muscovado sugar**
3 tablespoons **milk**
75 g (3 oz) **golden icing sugar**

Beat together the butter, sugar, flour and egg in a bowl until pale and creamy. Stir in the chopped nuts.

Divide the mixture evenly between 16 mini silicone muffin cases arranged on a baking sheet. Bake in a preheated oven, 180°C (350°F), Gas Mark 4, for 10–12 minutes or until risen and just firm. Leave to cool in the cases for 2 minutes, then transfer to a wire rack to cool completely.

Make the frosting. Heat the butter, muscovado sugar and milk in a saucepan until the sugar dissolves. Bring to the boil and boil for 1 minute until the mixture turns slightly syrupy. Remove from the heat and pour into a heatproof bowl. Sift the icing sugar into the bowl and beat until the mixture is smooth and fudge-like. Spread over the cakes and scatter with chopped peanuts.

For honey & pine nut cakes, toast and chop 100 g (3½ oz) pine nuts. Make the cakes as above, replacing the peanuts with half the pine nuts. For the syrup, put 25 g (1 oz) slightly salted butter, 1½ tablespoons clear honey and 1 tablespoon light muscovado sugar in a small saucepan, bring to the boil and cook until syrupy. Remove from the heat and stir in 1 tablespoon lemon juice and the remaining pine nuts. Spoon over the cakes and serve warm.

savoury bakes

blue cheese & thyme straws

Makes **40**
Preparation time **15 minutes**
Cooking time **15 minutes**

100 g (3½ oz) **plain flour**
2 teaspoons finely chopped **thyme**, plus extra for scattering
100 g (3½ oz) **unsalted butter**, chilled and diced
100 g (3½ oz) **firm blue cheese**, rind removed and grated
1 egg yolk
sea salt

Put the flour and thyme in a bowl or food processor. Add the butter and rub in with the fingertips or process until the mixture resembles breadcrumbs. Stir in the cheese and egg yolk and mix or blend to a dough.

Knead the dough on a lightly floured surface until smooth, then roll out to 5 mm (¼ inch) thick. Trim the edges and cut into sticks 5 mm (¼ inch) wide and about 9 cm (3½ inches) long. Place slightly apart on a greased baking sheet.

Sprinkle with sea salt and bake in a preheated oven, 200°C (400°F), Gas Mark 6, for about 15 minutes until golden. Leave to cool slightly on the sheet, then transfer to a wire rack to cool completely. Serve scattered with extra thyme.

For olive twists, roll out 375 g (12 oz) ready-made puff pastry on a lightly floured surface to a 25 x 15 cm (10 x 6 inch) rectangle and cut in half. Beat together 1 egg yolk and 1 tablespoon water, then brush thinly over one half. Spread thinly with 3 tablespoons black or green olive tapenade. Place the second piece on top and roll again to make a 24 cm (9 inch) square. Trim the edges and brush the surface with more of the egg yolk mixture. Cut the pastry in half, then cut each half across into 2 cm (¾ inch) strips. Twist each strip several times, then place on a lightly greased baking sheet. Sprinkle with sea salt and bake as above.

ham & tomato scones

Makes about **12**
Preparation time **20 minutes**
Cooking time **12–15 minutes**

125 ml (4 fl oz) **milk**, plus extra to glaze
2 tablespoons **sun-dried tomato paste**
50 g (2 oz) **Serrano ham**, finely diced
250 g (8 oz) **self-raising flour**
1 teaspoon **baking powder**
40 g (1½ oz) **butter**, chilled and diced
ground paprika, for sprinkling

Beat together the milk, tomato paste and ham in a jug. Put the flour and baking powder in a bowl or food processor. Add the butter and rub in with the fingertips or process until the mixture resembles fine breadcrumbs. Add the milk mixture and mix or blend briefly to a soft dough.

Shape the dough into a ball on a lightly floured surface, then roll out to 1.5 cm (¾ inch) thick. Cut out about 12 rounds using a 4 cm (1½ inch) plain biscuit cutter, re-rolling the trimmings to make more. Place slightly apart on a greased baking sheet, then lightly brush with milk and sprinkle with paprika.

Bake in a preheated oven, 220°C (425°F), Gas Mark 7, for 12–15 minutes or until risen and golden. Transfer to a wire rack to cool. Serve warm or cold, split and buttered with Chilli & Parsley Butter, if liked (see below).

For chilli & parsley butter, to serve as an accompaniment, beat together 100 g (3½ oz) softened slightly salted butter, ½ deseeded and finely chopped medium-strength red chilli, 2 tablespoons finely chopped parsley and 1 crushed garlic clove in a bowl. Turn into a small dish, cover and chill until ready to serve.

stilton & peppercorn scones

Makes about **12**
Preparation time **20 minutes**
Cooking time **12–15 minutes**

- 2 tablespoons **green peppercorns in brine**, rinsed and drained
- 125 g (4 oz) **plain wholemeal flour**
- 100 g (3½ oz) **self-raising flour**
- 2 teaspoons **baking powder**
- 50 g (2 oz) **slightly salted butter**, chilled and diced
- 50 g (2 oz) **Stilton cheese**, rind removed and grated
- 150 ml (¼ pint) **milk**, plus extra to glaze

Roughly crush the peppercorns using a pestle and mortar or a small bowl and the end of a rolling pin.

Put the flours and baking powder in a bowl or food processor. Add the butter and rub in with the fingertips or process until the mixture resembles fine breadcrumbs. Add the peppercorns, cheese and milk and mix or blend to a soft dough, adding a dash more milk if the dough feels dry.

Shape the dough into a ball on a lightly floured surface, then roll out to 1.5 cm (¾ inch) thick. Cut out about 12 rounds using a 4 cm (1½ inch) plain biscuit cutter, re-rolling the trimmings to make more. Place slightly apart on a greased baking sheet and lightly brush with milk.

Bake in a preheated oven, 220°C (425°F), Gas Mark 7, for 12–15 minutes or until risen and golden. Transfer to a wire rack to cool. Serve warm or cold, split and buttered, with Pear Relish, if liked (see below).

For pear relish, to serve as an accompaniment, mix together ½ finely chopped small red onion and 2 peeled, cored and finely chopped ripe pears in a bowl, then add 2 tablespoons chopped chives, 1 tablespoon caster sugar, 1 tablespoon white wine vinegar, a pinch of ground cloves and a little salt and pepper. Mix well, cover and leave to stand for at least 2 hours before serving with the scones.

bacon, thyme & potato muffins

Makes **12**
Preparation time **20 minutes**, plus cooling
Cooking time **15–20 minutes**

- 400 g (13 oz) **waxy potatoes**, peeled and diced
- 100 g (3½ oz) **smoked streaky bacon**, finely chopped
- 275 g (9 oz) **self-raising flour**
- 2 teaspoons **baking powder**
- 1 tablespoon chopped **thyme**, plus extra sprigs for scattering
- 175 ml (6 fl oz) **milk**
- 5 tablespoons **olive oil**
- 1 **egg**, beaten
- **salt** and **pepper**

Cook the potatoes in a saucepan of salted boiling water for 5–6 minutes until softened. Drain and leave to cool.

Heat a dry frying pan and fry the bacon until golden and crisp. Leave to cool.

Mix together the flour, baking powder, chopped thyme and a little salt and pepper in a bowl. Stir in the potatoes and bacon. Beat together the milk, oil and egg in a jug. Add to the dry ingredients and stir together using a large metal spoon until just combined.

Divide the mixture evenly between paper muffin cases arranged in a 12-hole muffin tray. Sprinkle with a little salt and scatter with thyme. Bake in a preheated oven, 220°C (425°F), Gas Mark 7, for 15–20 minutes until risen and golden. Transfer to a wire rack to cool. Serve warm or cold, scattered with extra thyme sprigs.

For sweet potato & coriander muffins, cook 400 g (13 oz) peeled and diced sweet potatoes as above instead of the waxy potatoes. Crush 1 teaspoon cumin seeds using a pestle and mortar or a small bowl and the end of a rolling pin. Make the muffins as above, omitting the bacon and thyme and adding the sweet potatoes, crushed cumin, 4 tablespoons chopped fresh coriander and 1 teaspoon salt to the dry ingredients. Bake as above.

sweetcorn & ham muffins

Makes **12**
Preparation time **15 minutes**
Cooking time **20 minutes**

175 g (6 oz) **frozen sweetcorn**
150 g (5 oz) **self-raising flour**
150 g (5 oz) **cornmeal**
2 teaspoons **baking powder**
75 g (3 oz) **Gruyère cheese**, grated
4 tablespoons **chopped chives**
100 g (3½ oz) **cooked ham hock**, diced
2 **eggs**, beaten
200 ml (7 fl oz) **milk**
4 tablespoons **vegetable oil**
salt and **pepper**

Cook the sweetcorn in a saucepan of boiling water for 1 minute. Drain well.

Mix together the flour, cornmeal, baking powder, cheese, chives and a little salt and pepper in a bowl. Stir in the ham and sweetcorn. Beat together the eggs, milk and oil in a jug. Add to the dry ingredients and stir together using a large metal spoon until just combined.

Divide the mixture evenly between paper muffin cases arranged in a 12-hole muffin tray. Bake in a preheated oven, 220°C (425°F), Gas Mark 7, for 20 minutes or until golden and just firm to the touch. Transfer to a wire rack to cool.

For roasted pepper muffins, halve, core and deseed 3 red peppers. Place on a foil-lined baking sheet and drizzle with 1 tablespoon olive oil. Roast in a preheated oven, 220°C (425°F), Gas Mark 7, for 45 minutes or until soft and beginning to char around the edges. Leave to cool, then roughly chop. Mix together 300 g (10 oz) self-raising flour, 1 teaspoon baking powder, 1 teaspoon celery salt, 75 g (3 oz) grated Cheddar cheese and plenty of freshly ground black pepper in a bowl. Beat together 3 eggs, 75 ml (3 fl oz) olive oil, 4 tablespoons pesto and 100 ml (3½ fl oz) milk in a jug. Add to the dry ingredients with the chopped peppers and continue as above.

parmesan & chive grissini

Makes about **30**
Preparation time **30 minutes**, plus proving
Cooking time **15–20 minutes**

- 500 g (1 lb) **strong white bread flour**
- 2 teaspoons **fast-action dried yeast**
- 1 teaspoon **salt**, plus extra for sprinkling
- 50 g (2 oz) **Parmesan cheese**, finely grated
- 4 tablespoons **chopped chives**
- 3 tablespoons **olive oil**
- 300 ml (½ pint) **hand-hot water**
- **semolina**, for sprinkling
- beaten **egg**, to glaze

Mix together the flour, yeast, salt, cheese and chives in a bowl. Add the oil and measurement water and mix to a dough, adding a dash more water if the dough feels dry.

Knead the dough on a floured surface for 10 minutes until smooth and elastic. Place in a lightly oiled bowl, cover with clingfilm and leave to rise in a warm place until doubled in size.

Sprinkle 2 lightly oiled baking sheets with semolina. Punch the dough to deflate it, then roll out on a floured surface to a 30 x 20 cm (12 x 8 inch) rectangle. Cut across into 1 cm (½ inch) strips, then stretch each one slightly and place on a baking sheet.

Brush with beaten egg and sprinkle with extra semolina. Bake in a preheated oven, 220°C (425°F), Gas Mark 7, for 15–20 minutes until golden. Transfer to a wire rack to cool. Best eaten freshly baked.

For salted pretzels, make the dough as above, omitting the cheese and chives and adding 2 teaspoons finely chopped rosemary. Divide the dough in half and roll out each piece to a 25 cm (10 inch) square. Cover with a tea towel and leave for 5 minutes. Cut the dough across into very thin strips. Take a strip of dough and place on the surface. Curve the ends round, then twist them together, pressing the ends down on the centre of the curve to shape a pretzel. Repeat with the remaining strips. Transfer to 2 lightly oiled baking sheets and bake as above. Meanwhile, heat 4 teaspoons sea salt, 1 tablespoon caster sugar and 2 tablespoons water in a saucepan until dissolved. Brush over the hot pretzels and sprinkle with extra sea salt.

seeded oatcakes

Makes **20**
Preparation time **15 minutes**
Cooking time **25 minutes**

125 g (4 oz) **medium oatmeal**
75 g (3 oz) **plain flour**
4 tablespoons **mixed seeds**, such as **poppy seeds**, **linseeds** and **sesame seeds**
½ teaspoon **celery salt** or **sea salt**
½ teaspoon **freshly ground black pepper**
50 g (2 oz) **unsalted butter**, chilled and diced
5 tablespoons **cold water**

Put the oatmeal, flour, seeds, salt and pepper in a bowl or food processor. Add the butter and rub in with the fingertips or process until the mixture resembles breadcrumbs. Add the measurement water and mix or blend to a firm dough, adding a little more water if the dough feels dry.

Roll out the dough on a lightly floured surface to 2.5 mm (⅛ inch) thick. Cut out 20 rounds using a 6 cm (2½ inch) plain or fluted biscuit cutter, re-rolling the trimmings to make more. Place slightly apart on a large greased baking sheet.

Bake in a preheated oven, 180°C (350°F), Gas Mark 4, for about 25 minutes until firm. Transfer to a wire rack to cool. Serve with cheese.

For crushed spice biscuits, crush ½ teaspoon cumin seeds, ½ teaspoon coriander seeds and ¼ teaspoon dried chilli flakes using a pestle and mortar or a small bowl and the end of a rolling pin. Finely chop 25 g (1 oz) ready-to-eat dried apricots. Make the biscuits as above, omitting the seeds and celery salt and adding the crushed spices and apricots. Serve with soft cheeses.

red onion & herb soda bread

Makes **1 loaf**
Preparation time **15 minutes**, plus standing
Cooking time **30 minutes**

- 325 ml (11 fl oz) **milk**, plus extra if required
- 1 tablespoon **lemon juice**
- 1 small **red onion**, finely chopped
- 1 **egg**, beaten
- 250 g (8 oz) **plain wholemeal flour**
- 250 g (8 oz) **plain white flour**, plus extra for dusting
- 2 teaspoons **salt**
- 1 teaspoon **bicarbonate of soda**
- 25 g (1 oz) **mixed herbs**, such as **parsley, chervil, dill** and **chives**, chopped
- 40 g (1½ oz) **butter**, diced

Mix together the milk and lemon juice in a jug and leave to stand for 5 minutes. Stir in the onion and egg.

Put the flours, salt and bicarbonate of soda in a separate bowl and stir in the herbs. Add the butter and rub in with the fingertips until the mixture resembles fine breadcrumbs. Pour the milk mixture into the bowl and mix to a dough, adding a little more milk if the dough feels dry.

Shape the dough into a ball on a lightly floured surface, then place on a greased baking sheet and flatten slightly. Dust generously with extra flour. Using a sharp knife, cut a 2.5 cm (1 inch) deep cross through the top of the dough.

Bake in a preheated oven, 200°C (400°F), Gas Mark 6, for about 30 minutes until risen and deep golden. The base of the bread should sound hollow when tapped. Transfer to a wire rack to cool.

For fennel & Gruyère soda buns, melt 25 g (1 oz) butter in a frying pan and gently fry 1 small finely chopped fennel bulb for about 5 minutes until softened. Make the dough as above, replacing the onion with the fennel and adding 75 g (3 oz) finely grated Gruyère cheese instead of the herbs. Divide the dough into 8 pieces and shape each into a ball. Space slightly apart on a greased baking sheet and dust with flour. Score the top of each and bake as above, reducing the cooking time to 15 minutes.

easy pissaladières

Makes **8**
Preparation time **20 minutes**, plus cooling
Cooking time **35 minutes**

4 tablespoons **olive oil**
4 **onions**, thinly sliced
1 tablespoon chopped **oregano**, plus extra leaves for scattering
500 g (1 lb) **ready-made puff pastry**
beaten **egg**, to glaze
75 g (3 oz) **pitted black olives**, halved
50 g (2 oz) can **anchovies**, drained
pepper

Heat the oil in a frying pan, add the onions and fry very gently for about 20 minutes until soft and golden. Stir in the chopped oregano and leave to cool.

Roll out the pastry on a lightly floured surface to a 65 x 30 cm (25½ x 12 inch) rectangle. Cut out 8 rounds by cutting around a 14 cm (5½ inch) bowl. Fold the edge of each pastry round over to form a thin rim, pressing the edge firmly down into the base to hold it in place.

Place on a large lightly oiled baking sheet and brush the edges with beaten egg. Stir the olives and a little pepper into the onion mixture and spread over the pastry bases. Halve the anchovies lengthways and then widthways, then arrange over the tops. Bake in a preheated oven, 200°C (400°F), Gas Mark 6, for 15 minutes until risen and golden. Serve warm or cold, scattered with oregano leaves.

For goats' cheese pithiviers, mix together 200 g (7 oz) soft goats' cheese, 3 crushed garlic cloves, 2 tablespoons chopped parsley, 1 tablespoon chopped mint and a little salt and pepper in a bowl. Roll out 500 g (1 lb) ready-made puff pastry and cut out eight 12 cm (5 inch) rounds using a plain biscuit cutter or by cutting around a small bowl. Brush the edges of half the rounds with beaten egg and spoon the filling into the centres. Cover with the remaining rounds, pressing the pastry down firmly around the edges. Transfer to an oiled baking sheet. Brush the tops with beaten egg, then score curved, shallow lines from the centres of the pastries. Bake as above for 20 minutes or until puffed and golden.

chilli & chorizo roly polys

Makes **30**
Preparation time **15 minutes**, plus cooling and freezing
Cooking time **20 minutes**

- 1 tablespoon **olive oil**
- ½ **medium-strength red chilli**, finely chopped
- 1 small **red onion**, finely chopped
- 75 g (3 oz) **chorizo**, finely chopped
- 2 tablespoons chopped **fresh coriander**
- 500 g (1 lb) **ready-made puff pastry**
- 1 **egg yolk**
- 2 teaspoons **water**
- **salt**

Heat the oil in a frying pan, add the chilli and onion and gently fry for 5 minutes until softened. Remove from the heat and leave to cool. Stir in the chorizo, coriander and a little salt.

Roll out the pastry on a lightly floured surface to a 40 x 30 cm (16 x 12 inch) rectangle. Mix the egg yolk with the measurement water and brush thinly over the pastry. Spread the chorizo mixture in an even layer on top. Roll up the pastry, starting from a long side. Wrap in clingfilm and freeze for 30 minutes.

Trim off the ends of the pastry log and cut across into 1 cm (½ inch) thick slices. Lay the slices on a floured surface and roll lightly with the rolling pin to flatten. Place on 2 greased baking sheets.

Brush with a little more of the egg yolk mixture and bake in a preheated oven, 220°C (425°F), Gas Mark 7, for 10 minutes. Press down the centres of the pastries using the back of a spoon if risen, then return to the oven and cook for a further 5 minutes or until golden. Transfer to a wire rack to cool slightly, then serve warm or cold.

For garlic & herb roly polys, beat together 100 g (3½ oz) cream cheese and 1 tablespoon olive oil in a bowl until the cheese has softened. Add 2 crushed garlic cloves, 4 tablespoons chopped parsley, 2 tablespoons chopped tarragon, a little salt and plenty of pepper. Shape the pastries as above, replacing the chorizo mixture with the garlic and herb cheese. Bake as above on baking sheets lined with baking parchment.

sunflower seed & rye bread

Makes **1 loaf**
Preparation time **10 minutes**
Cooking time **50 minutes**

200 g (7 oz) **plain flour**
200 g (7 oz) **wholemeal spelt flour**
100 g (3½ oz) **rye flour**
2 teaspoons **baking powder**
1 teaspoon **salt**
75 g (3 oz) **sunflower seeds**, plus 2 tablespoons
500 g (1 lb) **natural yogurt**
milk, to glaze

Mix together the flours, baking powder, salt and the 75 g (3 oz) sunflower seeds in a bowl. Stir in the yogurt and mix to a fairly soft dough.

Shape the dough into a log on a floured surface, then drop into a greased 1.25 kg (2½ lb) or 1.5 litre (2½ pint) loaf tin. Brush with a little milk and sprinkle with the remaining sunflower seeds.

Bake in a preheated oven, 220°C (425°F), Gas Mark 7, for 20 minutes. Reduce the oven temperature to 160°C (325°F), Gas Mark 3, and bake for a further 30 minutes. The base of the bread should sound hollow when tapped. If necessary, return to the oven for a little longer. Transfer to a wire rack to cool. Serve with cheese or Smoked Salmon Spread, if liked (see below).

For smoked salmon spread, to serve as an accompaniment, put 100 g (3½ oz) chopped smoked salmon trimmings and 250 g (8 oz) mascarpone cheese in a food processor and blend until smooth, scraping down the mixture from the side of the bowl. Add 4 tablespoons chopped dill, a squeeze of lemon or lime juice, plenty of black pepper and a little salt if needed. Blend lightly to mix. Turn into a small dish and serve with the bread and lemon or lime slices.

merguez sausage rolls

Makes **32**
Preparation time **25 minutes**
Cooking time **25–30 minutes**

500 g (1 lb) **good-quality pork sausagemeat**
2 teaspoons **ground cumin**
2 teaspoons **ground coriander**
2 teaspoons **fennel seeds**
1 tablespoon **ground paprika**
2 **garlic cloves**, crushed
2 **spring onions**, finely chopped
500 g (1 lb) **ready-made puff pastry**
beaten **egg**, to glaze
salt and **pepper**

Put the sausagemeat in a bowl and add the cumin, coriander, fennel seeds, paprika, garlic, spring onions and a little salt and pepper. Mix well with your hands until evenly combined.

Roll out the pastry thinly on a lightly floured surface to a 40 cm (16 inch) square, then cut into 4 strips. Divide the pork mixture into 4 pieces and pinch out a quarter of the sausagemeat along the centre of each strip.

Brush the pastry edges with a little beaten egg and fold one side of the pastry over the sausagemeat, pressing the edges of the pastry firmly together to make long, thin logs. Brush with beaten egg and cut into 5 cm (2 inch) lengths. Place on a large greased baking sheet and score 2 or 3 cuts along the top of each with a sharp knife.

Bake in a preheated oven, 220°C (425°F), Gas Mark 7, for 15 minutes. Reduce the temperature to 160°C (325°F), Gas Mark 3, and cook for a further 10–15 minutes until deep golden and cooked through.

For spicy satay rolls, mix together 400 g (13 oz) minced chicken or turkey, 50 g (2 oz) fresh white breadcrumbs, 2 crushed garlic cloves, 6 tablespoons crunchy peanut butter, 50 g (2 oz) grated creamed coconut, 1 tablespoon light muscovado sugar, 2 teaspoons mild curry paste, ½ teaspoon dried chilli flakes and a little salt in a bowl. Make the rolls as above, replacing the merguez mixture with the satay mixture.

index

acknowledgements

Executive editor: Eleanor Maxfield
Managing editor: Clare Churly
Designer: Eoghan O'Brien
Layout designer: Penny Stock
Photographer: William Shaw
Home economist: Joanna Farrow
Props stylist: Kim Sullivan
Senior production controller: Caroline Alberti

Special photography: © Octopus Publishing Group Limited/William Shaw
Other photography: Octopus Publishing Group/ Stephen Conroy 45, 95, 99, 101, 189; Will Heap 18, 58, 73, 97, 152, 167, 171, 173, 207; David Munns 6, 17 below, 20, 84; Lis Parsons 17 above, 41, 47, 119, 133, 185; William Shaw 43, 49, 75, 77, 93, 122, 151, 165, 178, 208; Ian Wallace 109, 183.